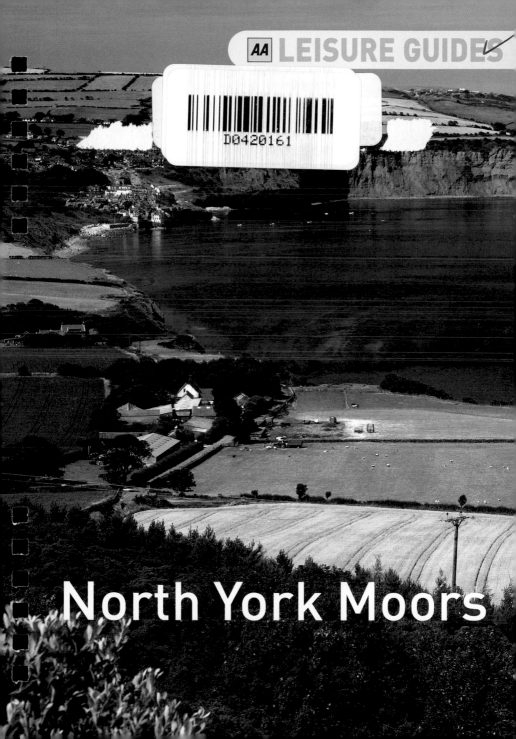

AA LEISURE GUIDES

D0420161

North York Moors

Author: John Morrison
Verifier: David Winpenny
Publisher: David Watchus
Managing Editor: Katey Mackenzie
Senior Editor: Sandy Draper
Senior Designers: Alison Fenton and Kat Mead
Page Layout: Liz Baldin of Bookwork
Picture Library Manager: Liz Allen
Picture Research: Kathy Lockley
Cartographic Editor: Jenny Wood of Skelley Cartographic Services
Cartographic Production: Geoff Chapman, Samantha Chalkley-Johnston and Graham Jones
Copy-editors: Marilynne Lanng of Bookwork and Pamela Stagg
Proofreader: Stephanie Smith
Internal Repro: Sarah Butler, Ian Little and Michael Moody
Index: Hilary Bird

Produced by AA Publishing
© Automobile Association Developments Limited 2007
Reprinted 2007

All rights reserved. No part of this publication may be reproduced, stored in a retrieval system, or
transmitted in any form or by any means – electronic, photocopying, recording or otherwise – unless
the written permission of the publishers has been obtained beforehand.

Published by AA Publishing (a trading name of Automobile Association Developments Limited, whose
registered office is Fanum House, Basing View, Basingstoke, Hampshire RG21 4EA; registered number
1878835).

 This product includes mapping data licensed from the Ordnance Survey® with the
permission of the Controller of Her Majesty's Stationery Office.
© Crown copyright 2007. All rights reserved. Licence number 100021153.

A03366

ISBN-10: 0-7495-5017-1
ISBN-13: 978-0-7495-5017-2

A CIP catalogue record for this book is available from the British Library.

The contents of this book are believed correct at the time of printing. Nevertheless, the publishers
cannot be held responsible for any errors or omissions or for changes in the details given in this book
or for the consequences of any reliance on the information it provides. We have tried to ensure
accuracy in this book, but things do change and would be grateful if readers would advise us of any
inaccuracies they may encounter. This does not affect your statutory rights.

We have taken all reasonable steps to ensure that the walks and cycle rides in this book are safe and
achievable by people with a realistic level of fitness. However, all outdoor activities involve a degree of
risk and the publishers accept no responsibility for any injuries caused to readers whilst following
these walks and cycle rides. For advice on walking and cycling in safety, see pages 16–17.

Some of the walks and cycle rides may appear in other AA books and publications.

Visit AA Publishing's website www.theAA.com/travel

Colour reproduction by Keenes, Andover
Printed in C&C Offset Printing, China

CONTENTS

CARDONALD COLLEGE LIBRARY

L | 914 | N o R | 3230181403
284 604

■ HAWNBY & EASTERSIDE HILL

Welcome to the...
North York Moors

The word 'moors' conjures up the image of a bleak, lonely and windswept landscape? Not the North York Moors. From the sharp escarpments in the west to the towering cliffs and sandy beaches on the east coast, the Moors offers a rich variety of landscapes, and attractions to please everyone.

The heart of the North York Moors – designated a National Park more fifty years ago – is the plateau of hills that glow with a soft-purple wash of heather in the late summer. This is England's largest expanse of heather, and one of the must-see sights. You can walk for miles along old drovers' tracks that will take you past mysterious ancient earthworks and mounds and the medieval moorland crosses that are a familiar feature of the 'tops'.

Thrusting into this high land are deep and densely wooded valleys, including Bransdale, with some of the area's remote farming communities; Farndale, famous for wild daffodils; and Rosedale, with remnants of iron working in a divine setting. Many of the area's most attractive towns and villages, such as Hutton-le-Hole and Lastingham, lie in the valleys.

Southwest of the central moorland are the more gentle Howardian Hills, where picturesque abbeys – Rievaulx and Byland – and ruined castles like Helmsley rise from wooded valleys. North again around the curve of the Cleveland Hills, villages like Swainby and Great Ayton – where Captain Cook was schooled – huddle beneath the humpbacks of the hills.

Deep forests occupy much of the southeastern quarter of the area, with walks, mountain-bike trails and picnic sites set out among the trees. And strung along the glorious coast, from Staithes to Scarborough, are some of Britain's highest cliffs, coves where smugglers landed contraband, idyllic fishing villages that appear to tumble headlong into the waves, and bracing headlands. Whitby, with its abbey, quirky church, Dracula connections and memories of its whaling past, is fascinating, while Scarborough lives up to its name as 'Queen of the Coast' with everything for a traditional, seaside family holiday, from beaches to a huge castle just asking to be explored.

Whether you're an adventurer or a potterer, a walker, a cyclist or a driver, the North York Moors has something to offer. And if you're looking for peace and quiet, that is as plentiful here as fresh air, too – just as it was during the 12th century when St Aelred, Abbot of Rievaulx, wrote that it offers 'a marvellous freedom from the tumult of the world'.

NORTH SEA

ESK DALE & NORTH

North York Moors

Esk Dale

WESTERN MOORS

CENTRAL MOORS

EASTERN MOORS & COAST

North Riding Forest Park

North Riding Forest Park

6 Walk start point

1 Cycle start point

2 Tour start point

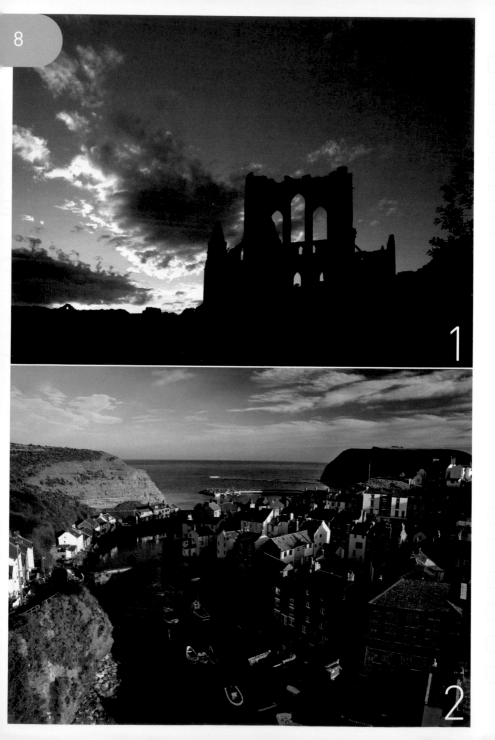

1

2

ESSENTIAL SPOTS

Enjoy the superb views across the Vale of York from the top of Sutton Bank...walk part (or all!) of the Cleveland Way, which starts at Helmsley and ends at Filey Brigg on the coast...visit Staithes, a perfect example of an old Yorkshire fishing village...search Whitby's many antique shops for jet or watch it being made in the craftsmens' workshops. hunt for a small carved mouse, Robert Thompson's unique trademark, on the furniture in local churches and visit the workshops at Kilburn...admire the thousands of daffodils at Farndale in springtime... linger by the extensive remains of Rievaulx Abbey... steam along the rails on the North Yorkshire Moors Railway, which runs from Pickering to Grosmont...look out for the stone crosses that litter the moors...walk along the Roman road in Wheeldale in the footsteps of Roman soldiers...take the scenic Newtondale Forest Drive through North Riding Forest.

1 **Rievaulx Abbey**
The magnificent ruins of Rievaulx Abbey, set in a splendid wooded valley of the River Rye.

2 **Staithes**
The village of Stalthes is a delight to explore. Its position, wedged between steep-sided cliffs and Cowbar Beck, resulted in an attractive jumble of house building.

3 **Hutton-le-Hole**
Neat, flower-bedecked houses of mellow local stone, grouped around a tidy green that extends the length of the village, make Hutton-le-Hole a candidate for the title of Yorkshire's prettiest village.

3

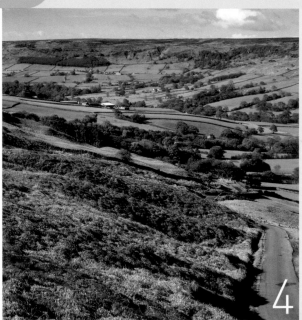

4 Farndale

The remote valley of Farndale, with its maze of narrow winding lanes and patchwork of fields, is where you can experience moorland scenery at its most beautiful.

5 Egton Bridge

A tranquil corner at Egton Bridge. This pretty little village is set the lush woodland of the Esk Valley.

6 Robin Hood's Bay

The pretty litlle fishing village of Robin Hood's Bay is a tumble of brightly painted cottages that seem to stagger their way along the narrow roads towards the sea.

7 Stone Crosses

Young Ralph Cross, standing tall at a junction of roads near Rosedale Head, is the symbol of the North York Moors National Park. It is just one of many ancient stones and crosses found on these moors.

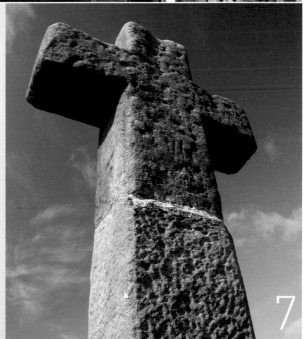

DAY ONE

For many people a weekend break or a long weekend is a popular way of spending their leisure time. These four pages offer a loosely planned itinerary designed to ensure that you make the most of your time, whatever the weather, and see and enjoy the very best of the area.

Friday Night

Stay at the Feversham Arms, Helmsley. This is a charming hotel located just a few yards from the Market Square with its own swimming pool and luxurious four-poster beds in many of the rooms. The restaurant is renowned for its good food (especially shellfish and game in season) and outstanding wine list.

Saturday Morning

Your first stop should be the local Tourist Information Centre, located in the castle, for details of any events that may be happening at the weekend.

Just a short drive north from Helmsley, on the B1257, you'll find the fascinating remains of Rievaulx Abbey to explore, one of Yorkshire's architectural gems, in a splendid setting in the valley of the River Rye.

Minor roads (make sure you have an atlas to hand) lead southwest to the fine Yorkshire village of Kilburn. Beneath the distinctive hill figure of the White Horse is the showroom of Robert Thompson's Craftsmen, whose work keeps alive the tradition and artistry of the famous 'Mouseman'. Opposite to the showroom is the visitor centre.

Saturday Lunch

Drive the short distance eastwards to the picturesque Byland Abbey where, directly opposite the ruins, you'll find the Abbey Inn. The stone-flagged floor, antique furniture and imaginative menu make this the ideal place for lunch.

Saturday Afternoon

Pass Helmsley once again and continue east along the A170 to Pickering, the terminus of the North Yorkshire Moors Railway. This preserved line offers a nostalgic return to the age of steam. A round trip to Goathland will show you some of the finest scenery in the North York Moors National Park, as well as giving you time to explore the moorland village perhaps now best known as a location for the TV series *Heartbeat*.

On your return to Pickering, drive north up the A169, passing the huge natural amphitheatre known as the Hole of Horcum, towards the port of Whitby.

Saturday Night

Three miles (4.8km) north of the town, off the A171, is Dunsley Hall Hotel, an impressive Victorian mansion in the quiet village of Dunsley where you can escape from the crowds.

HELMSLEY

WEEKEND AWAY

RUNSWICK BAY

DANBY DALE

DAY TWO

Our second and final day starts with a visit to the bustling resort of Whitby and a nearby picturesque fishing village, before driving along the beautiful Esk Valley and across the moors, passing through a number of lovely villages, before arriving back in Helmsley.

Sunday Morning

Explore Whitby on foot. It's a fascinating town, with surprises at every turn in its winding streets. The abbey, St Mary's Church, the Captain Cook Museum and the harbour are just a few of the 'musts'.

On a different scale are the tiny fishing villages of Staithes (north of Whitby) and Robin Hood's Bay (a few miles to the south). Both are achingly picturesque; take time to explore one or the other.

Afterwards, a leisurely drive along the beautiful Esk Valley, passing the lovely of villages of Grosmont, Glaisdale (look out for the Beggar's Bridge) and Lealholm will bring you to Danby. At the Moors Centre you can learn how the moorland landscape came to look the way it does, and perhaps have a coffee.

Drive south from Danby, along Blakey Ridge (this is on an unclassified road, more map reading needed). With the valley of Rosedale to your left and Farndale to your right, this is moorland scenery at its very best.

Sunday Lunch

Look out for the Lion Inn, miles from anywhere on Blakey Ridge, where travellers have long received a warm welcome. Our suggested itinerary should make this a late lunch. No problem, the Lion Inn serves its excellent meals throughout the day.

Sunday Afternoon

Continue driving along Blakey Ridge, with perhaps a moorland walk to fill the lungs with pure upland air. Look out for the guide stones on the roadside. The road brings you to Hutton-le-Hole, one of Yorkshire's picture-postcard villages and well worth exploring. Near by is the equally pretty Lastingham.

Our weekend started with one monastic gem and ends with another intriguing religious site. The church at Lastingham has a 'secret' crypt, built almost a thousand years ago.

Drive west along the A170 to arrive back in Helmsley where you can enjoy some afternoon tea before heading for home.

Route facts

MINIMUM TIME The time stated for completing each route is the estimated minimum time that a reasonably fit family group of walkers or cyclists would take to complete the circuit. This does not allow for rest or refreshment stops.

OS MAP Each route is shown on a map. However, some detail is lost because of the restrictions imposed by scale, so for this reason, we recommend that you use the maps in conjunction with a more detailed Ordnance Survey map. The relevant map for each walk or cycle ride is listed.

START This indicates the start location and parking area. This is a six-figure grid reference prefixed by two letters showing which 62.5-mile (100km) square of the National Grid it refers to. You'll find more information on grid references on most Ordnance Survey maps.

CYCLE HIRE We list, within reason, the nearest cycle hire shop/centre.

❶ Here we highlight any potential difficulties or dangers along the cycle ride or walk. If a particular route is suitable for older, fitter children we say so here. Also, we give guidelines of a route's suitability for younger children, for example the symbol 8+ indicates that the route can probably be attempted by children aged 8 years and above.

Walks & Cycle Rides

Each walk and cycle ride has a panel giving information for the walker and cyclist, including the distance, terrain, nature of the paths, and where to park your car.

WALKING

All of the walks are suitable for families, but less experienced family groups, especially those with younger children, should try the shorter walks. Route finding is usually straightforward, but the maps are for guidance only and we recommend that you always take the relevant Ordnance Survey map with you.

Risks

Although each walk has been researched with a view to minimising any risks, no walk in the countryside can be considered to be completely free from risk. Walking in the outdoors will always require a degree of common sense and judgement to ensure that it is as safe as possible, especially for young children.
• Be particularly careful on cliff paths and in upland terrain, where the consequences of a slip can be serious.
• Remember to check tidal conditions before walking on the seashore.
• Some sections of route are by, or cross, busy roads.

Remember traffic is a danger even on minor country lanes.
• Be careful around farmyard machinery and livestock.
• Be prepared for the consequences of changes in the weather and check the forecast before you set out.
• Ensure the whole family is properly equipped, wearing suitable clothing and a good pair of boots or sturdy walking shoes. Take waterproof clothing with you and a torch if you are walking in the winter months.
• Remember the weather can change quickly at any time of the year, and in moorland and heathland areas, mist and fog can make route-finding much harder. In summer, take account of the heat and sun by wearing a hat, sunscreen and carrying enough water.
• On walks away from centres of population you should carry a mobile phone, whistle and, if possible, a survival bag. If you do have an accident requiring emergency services, make a note of your position as accurately as possible and dial 999.

CYCLING

In devising the cycle rides in this guide, every effort has been made to use designated cycle paths, or to link them with quiet country lanes and waymarked byways and bridleways. In a few cases, some fairly busy B-roads have been used to join up with quieter routes.

Rules of the road

• Ride in single file on narrow and busy roads.

• Be alert, look and listen for traffic, especially on narrow lanes and blind bends, and be extra careful when descending steep hills, as loose gravel or a poor road surface can lead to an accident.

• In wet weather make sure that you keep an appropriate distance between you and other riders.

• Make sure you indicate your intentions clearly.

• Brush up on *The Highway Code* before venturing out on to the road.

Off-road safety code of conduct

• Only ride where you know it is legal to do so. Cyclists are not allowed to cycle on public footpaths, marked in yellow. The only 'rights of way' open to cyclists are bridleways (blue markers) and unsurfaced tracks, known as byways, which are open to all traffic and waymarked in red.

• Canal towpaths: you need a permit to cycle on some stretches of towpath (www.waterscape.com). Remember that access paths can be steep and slippery so always push your bike under low bridges and by locks.

• Always yield to walkers and horses, giving adequate warning of your approach.

• Don't expect to cycle at high speeds.

• Keep to the main trail to avoid any unnecessary erosion to the area beside the trail and to prevent skidding, especially in wet weather conditions.

• Remember to follow the Country Code.

Preparing your bicycle

Check the wheels, tyres, brakes and cables. Lubricate hubs, pedals, gear mechanisms and cables. Make sure you have a pump, a bell, a rear rack to carry panniers and a set of lights.

Equipment

• A cycling helmet provides essential protection.

• Make sure you are visible to other road users, by wearing light-coloured or luminous clothing in daylight and sashes or reflective strips in failing light and darkness.

• Take extra clothes with you, depending on the season, and a wind/waterproof jacket.

• Carry a basic tool kit, a pump, a strong lock and a first aid kit.

• Always carry enough water for your outing.

Walk Map Legend

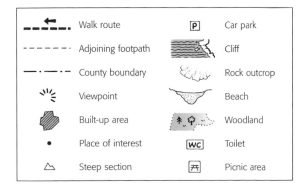

←	Walk route	P	Car park
- - - - -	Adjoining footpath		Cliff
— · — · —	County boundary		Rock outcrop
⁄⁄	Viewpoint		Beach
	Built-up area		Woodland
•	Place of interest	WC	Toilet
△	Steep section	🎪	Picnic area

Esk Dale & North

INTRODUCTION

The River Esk meanders enticingly from its source on the moorlands near to Westerdale, linking a number of lovely villages before reaching the North Sea with a flourish and dividing the fascinating fishing port of Whitby into two. The National Park's Visitor Centre, which is located close to Esk, near Danby, is the perfect spot to enjoy a picnic or a riverside stroll as well as learn about the unique moorland habitats of the National Park. A little way downstream there is an arched packhorse bridge, intriguingly named Duck Bridge over the Esk. From source to sea you will find that the River Esk holds many delights; the valley road between Stokesley and Whitby crosses and re-crosses it many times. Rail travellers follow its course more closely on the scenic line between Middlesbrough and Whitby. But the best way to see Esk Dale is on foot. The Esk Valley Walk is a waymarked route, which begins at Castleton and follows the river and the villages that lie along its banks, to the golden coast at Whitby.

1 Walk start point

1 Tour start point

LEALHOLM

DANBY DALE

Unmissable attractions

Admire the fantastic views from Roseberry Topping...explore the many twists and turns of Whitby's bustling historic streets...visit the fascinating Moors Centre near Danby and discover what makes the North York Moors such a special place...cycle along the minor roads between Castleton, Danby and Lealholm in the Esk Valley... visit Egton Bridge in August and experience the famous Gooseberry Show...drive the high road over Castleton Rigg and enjoy moorland scenery at its best...admire the gleaming old locomotives getting up steam at Grosmont station...enjoy the splendid wooded surroundings of Gisborough Hall...get some sea air at Runswick – one of the loveliest sandy bays on the Yorkshire Coast.

1

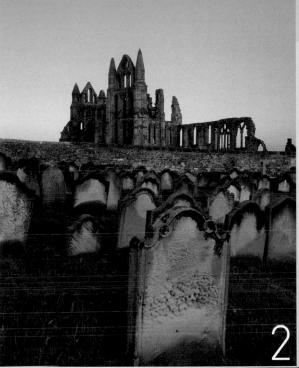

1 Roseberry Topping
The distinctive shape of Roseberry Topping, seen here looming up out of the mist, gained its distinctive profile after intensive iron-stone mining caused a huge landslip in 1921.

2 Whitby Abbey
Perched high on the clifftop east of Whitby are the magnificent ruins of Whitby Abbey.

3 Sandsend
The pretty village of Sandsend is set against a backdrop of cliffs at the northern end of a long arc of sandy beach.

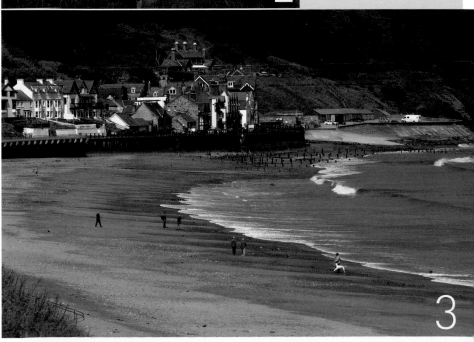

CASTLETON   MAP REF NZ6807

The castle is long gone from Castleton; only the name and a mound to the north of the village remain – unsentimentally, a lot of the stone from the ruined castle was probably recycled and used to build Danby Castle. Castleton used to have regular markets and a goods yard on the railway; the markets have gone, but the village still has its passenger station on the Esk Valley railway line.

The River Esk, which rises at Esklets in Westerdale to the south, is joined at Castleton by a tributary, Commondale Beck. To the north of the village is an expanse of moorland, but the landscape is very different from that of the south, with a selection of minor roads, tracks and footpaths exploring a landscape of great variety. Two routes 'take the high road' over Castleton Rigg, enjoying panoramic views down into Westerdale and Danby Dale, and on to Ralph Cross (used as the National Park emblem) and the head of beautiful Rosedale. This is moorland scenery at its best; valley bottoms divided up into neat fields by drystone walls, the pattern interrupted by little copses.

■ Insight

MOORLAND 'INTAKES'

You'll probably notice a sudden contrast where the fields stop and open moorland begins, showing that the fields higher up the valley sides are 'intakes' – land 'taken in' from the moorland above. At the head of several moorland valleys are ruined farmsteads, which were abandoned when the living became too precarious. Here you will often see unmanaged grassy pasture reverting back to heather and bracken.

You would probably hesitate to call Commondale, northwest of Castleton on the Esk Valley line, one of the prettier villages on the moors. This scattering of houses and farms occupies a hillside overlooking Commondale Moor. The village's most striking aspect is the use of brick, as much as stone, as a building material – the diminutive brick-built Church of St Peter, in particular, stands out like the proverbial sore thumb. The reason is very simple: until the 1950s Commondale had its own brickworks here, and bricks and tiles form vital decorative elements in a number of houses throughout the village, and on the façade of the old Co-op shop.

The village name was once written as 'Colmandale'. It is said that Colman, Bishop of Lindisfarne, stopped off here on his travels to Whitby Abbey.

DANBY   MAP REF NZ7008

The lovely village of Danby lies on a crossroads; blink and you've missed it. But it was to this little village that John Atkinson came, at the age of 36, as minister of the parish. He was Essex-born and until the end of his long life retained the natural curiosity of the newcomer. One of his major passions was prehistory, and the moors – with their burial mounds, standing stones and wayside crosses – provided much to excite his inquiring mind. He died in 1900, and is buried in the churchyard.

There are a number of interesting features in the immediate vicinity, and the easiest way to see them is to park at the National Park's Visitor Centre, just half a mile (800m) from the village on the road to Lealholm. The Moors Centre represents the public face of the National Park. Here you can discover what makes the North York Moors so special and the unique habitats that the moors supports. The building that houses the Moors Centre was once a shooting lodge for the Dawnay family, who bought the Manor of Danby in 1656; it now hosts exhibitions and a wide variety of events, including guided walks. The evolution of the moorland landscape is explained, and those whose needs extend no further than a mug of tea and a slice of cake are equally well catered for. The Moors Centre sits in 13 acres (5.2ha) of land, close to the Esk, a lovely spot to enjoy a picnic or a stroll along the riverside. A number of waymarked walks explore the immediate environs; longer walks start from the car park.

Just a little way downstream is the intriguingly named Duck Bridge. This superb late 14th-century example of an arched packhorse bridge is a tangible reminder of a time when sturdy ponies, laden down with twin pannier bags, were the main means by which goods and sundries were transported.

The packhorse trail leads towards Danby Castle, once a fortified house of distinction, though most of the medieval stonework has since been incorporated into a farmhouse; there is only limited public access. The castle, built in the 14th century, was once the home of Catherine Parr, the sixth wife of Henry VIII, who fared better than his other wives and, indeed, survived him. Past Danby Castle Farm the road goes through a minor valley; Little Fryup Dale.

■ Activity

CYCLING IN THE ESK VALLEY

The minor roads between Castleton, Danby and Lealholm in the Esk Valley are ideal for cycling as they are quiet and the valley floor level. With a little help from the OS Landranger map Sheet 94 1:50,000 it is possible to avoid most of the steep gradients on the roads out of the valley.

EGTON BRIDGE MAP REF NZ8004

Egton and Egton Bridge are two villages separated by both the River Esk and a steep descent. Egton has nothing to do with eggs; it appeared in the Domesday Book as Egetune, meaning 'the town of the oak trees'. The oaks are gone, as are the annual hiring fairs, when farmers would look to employ farm labourers for the forthcoming year. Even the weekly markets, for which the village was granted a charter by William of Orange, are no longer held in the village's broad street. But the village is important as the venue, every August, for one of the area's largest agricultural shows.

A new bridge, built in 1993, spans the River Esk at Egton Bridge. The stone arch replaces an ugly metal structure that was itself merely a replacement for the original bridge, which was swept away in floods in the 1930s.

Egton Bridge was the birthplace in 1599 of Father Nicholas Postgate, who ministered to his Catholic flock at much danger to himself. For the 'crime' of baptising a child into the Catholic faith, Father Postgate was sent for trial at York. In 1678 he was subjected – he was in his 80s – to the ultimate punishment,

EGTON BRIDGE

being hanged, drawn and quartered. In remaining staunchly Roman Catholic, Egton Bridge became known as 'the village missed by the Reformation'. The impressive Catholic Church of St Hedda contains relics of Father Postgate's ministry. Half-way up the hill to Egton is a house with a tiny chapel hidden in the roof, reached by a secret passage. The room was rediscovered 150 years after Postgate's death, since when the house has been known as the Mass House.

Every year, in August, the famous Egton Bridge Gooseberry Show is held. You will have to be a spectator rather than a competitor – at least until you are voted in as a member of the Old Gooseberry Society, founded in 1800. Size, not taste, is what matters here.

Ramblers alight at Egton Bridge, a stop on the Middlesbrough to Whitby line, and walk along the Esk Valley to Lealholm to catch the next train home.

GLAISDALE MAP REF NZ7705

Glaisdale is a straggle of little houses clinging to the hillside overlooking the River Esk. Ironstone was worked here; for a time the Angler's Arms was known as the Three Blastfurnaces. However, the Glaisdale mines were never as productive as those of nearby Rosedale.

The valley is very steep-sided here, and even with the benefit of hairpin bends motorists have to negotiate the 1-in-3 gradient of Limber Hill on their way up to Egton with care.

The area is criss-crossed old tracks – a relic of a time when Glaisdale was an important trading centre. Through East Arncliff Wood the route is still marked by a line of causeway stones. A number of these paths converge on Beggar's Bridge, a packhorse bridge with a romantic story.

It was not easy to cross the Esk at the time when Tom Ferris was courting a local lass who lived on the opposite side of the river. If Tom was not actually a beggar, he was certainly a man of few means. He hoped to win the hand of his beloved by bettering his position, so he enlisted on a ship that was setting out from Whitby to fight against the Spanish Armada, or, as some say, as a privateer.

When he tried to say farewell to the lady, however, he was thwarted by the River Esk in spate. He sought fame and fortune, and became a very successful merchant and Lord Mayor of Hull. Yet he never forgot Glaisdale, and erected the splendid arch of Beggar's Bridge so that no other young lovers should be needlessly parted.

GREAT AYTON MAP REF NZ5610

Great Ayton is bisected by the River Leven, whose clear waters seem almost to deny that the industrial heartland of Middlesbrough is just a short drive away. Behind Great Ayton is the famous profile of Roseberry Topping (1,056 feet/322m), the conical peak, a distinctive landmark for miles around.

Great Ayton has two churches that lie almost side by side. All Saints' Church is a delightful building dating back to the 12th century, though additions have been made in every succeeding century. The original tower was demolished in 1880. The interior is quite simple, with walls of rough-hewn stone, and enough

■ Visit

POSTGATE SCHOOL

Founded in 1704, the school in Great Ayton was designed to take eight poor boys of the town, but was soon accommodating up to 30 boys and girls. The school fees for the young James Cook were paid for by the lord of the manor, Thomas Skottowe, who employed Cook's father. The school is now home to the fascinating Captain Cook Schoolroom Museum.

■ Insight

THE RAIL TRAIL

The Rail Trail extends from Grosmont to Goathland, so it can be combined with a trip along this most scenic of railway lines (the Rail Trail booklet suggests the train journey to Goathland followed by a walk back to Grosmont). The 3-mile (4.8km) footpath follows the route of the original section of line between the two villages, via Beck Hole, as laid in 1836.

■ Visit

RIVER CROSSINGS

Beggar's Bridge at Glaisdale, built in 1619, is now used by walkers; cars cross by a metal bridge, while trains on the scenic Esk Valley line pass almost overhead on a viaduct. Here, within the space of a few yards, much of the transport history of the last few centuries is represented.

original architectural detail to keep most lovers of old churches engrossed.

The population of Great Ayton grew to the point where the congregation could no longer squeeze into this atmospheric building. Christ Church was consecrated as the new parish church in 1877; fortunately the old church escaped the fate of so many redundant churches, and is now open to the public during the summer months. James Cook's mother and five of his brothers and sisters are buried in churchyard.

GROSMONT MAP REF NZ8305

Built largely to house those who worked on the Pickering–Whitby railway line that splits the village in two, Grosmont was originally, and unimaginatively, called 'Tunnel'. With its terraced houses and mining spoil, Grosmont presents a more industrial face to the world than the other villages of the Esk Valley. Indeed, it was while excavating the Pickering-to-Whitby line, in 1835, that the richest ironstone deposits were first discovered. Once completed, the railway was a convenient method of ironstone delivery to ships in Whitby harbour. By the middle of the 19th century, Grosmont was a major supplier of ironstone to the ironmasters' furnaces on the Rivers Tyne and Tees.

The name 'Grosmont' recalls the 13th-century Grandmontine Priory, founded here by French monks. The priory is long gone, its place taken by Priory Farm and its stonework salvaged for secular buildings.

The Pickering–Whitby line was built in 1836 after consulting with George Stephenson, who came to the project straight from the triumphant success of his Stockton–Darlington railway. The line was closed, controversially, in 1965 by Beeching's infamous axe. It was reborn eight years later, thanks to massive support by railway enthusiasts, as the North Yorkshire Moors Railway, a recreational line manned by volunteers. There is nothing amateurish about the enterprise, though, for they maintain a regular timetable, come rain, shine, and even leaves on the line.

Railway buffs can spend some time admiring the gleaming old locomotives at Grosmont station, which has been convincingly restored to how it may it probably looked a century ago; there is also public access to the engine sheds.

Grosmont is the northern terminus of the railway, offering connections with main line services on the Esk Valley line between Middlesbrough and Whitby. It is a junction of roads and rivers, too, with the Murk Esk draining into the Esk.

GUISBOROUGH MAP REF NZ6015

Guisborough's broad main street and cobbled verges indicate that markets have been held here for centuries. The old market cross is topped by a sundial. Today the market traders put up their stalls on Thursdays and Saturdays, drawing their customers from many of the villages on the edge of the moors.

Like its close neighbour, Stokesley, the town's status has changed in recent years. Until the boundary changes of 1974, Guisborough was the capital town of the Cleveland district, which formed part of the North Riding of Yorkshire. Those reorganisations shifted the town into the county of Cleveland, but it is now back in North Yorkshire.

Beyond the main street and the market cross is the largely 15th-century Church of St Nicholas, where a cenotaph reinforces the links between the local de Bruce family and the Bruces of Scotland.

Robert the Bruce's grandfather is buried near by at Gisborough Priory.

The huge east window of the ruined Augustinian priory still stands to its full height of nearly 71 feet (20m), gazing out across farmland. To wander around the evocative ruins is to escape the bustle of Guisborough's busy streets. The priory was built in the early 14th century by Robert de Brus, who was related to the Scottish king, Robert the Bruce. In their contemplation of the life to come, the monks did not neglect to lay up their treasures on earth, and by the time of the Dissolution they had become one of the richest communities in the north.

Nearby you'll find Gisborough Hall, now a luxury hotel, sits in beautiful wooded surroundings. The original hall was built by Sir Thomas Challoner, whose son began the mining of alum on the moors in about 1600. The industry proved to be vital to the moorland economy for the following three centuries. Challoner stole the secrets of alum mining and processing from the Pope, no less, who had enjoyed a near-monopoly in the alum industry. He even persuaded some of the Pope's miners to accompany him back to England to begin alum mining on the moors. For this impertinence the Challoner family was excommunicated from the Catholic Church.

Just a mile (1.6km) out of town, on the A173 in the direction of Skelton, is Tocketts Mill. The water of Tocketts Beck still turns the waterwheel of this fine old flour-mill, and on certain milling days the building is open to the public.

KETTLENESS & GOLDSBOROUGH

MAP REF **NZ8414**

Travellers on the A174 between Staithes and Whitby are seldom tempted to take one of the roads to the left, before they arrive in the roadside village of Lythe. The signpost indicates Goldsborough and Kettleness, a pair of hamlets whose history is by no means as tranquil as they appear today.

The handful of houses clustered together in Kettleness look as if they could fall off the cliff top at any minute. That's precisely what happened in 1829, when a landslip devastated the entire community. Fortunately, the villagers had enough warning of the impending disaster to vacate their homes and businesses and were rescued by a ship waiting for them offshore. But you may wonder, why bother to rebuild the village on such an exposed site? The answer can be found by taking a path down on to Kettleness Point, a barren and rocky promontory. Here are the remains of productive alum mines where alum was shovelled out of the cliffs.

How precarious a living alum mining provided can be appreciated by the fact that the foundations of a large number of the mining buildings end suddenly at the cliff edge. The folk of Kettleness lost their livelihood, and their village, in the landslip of 1829; however, mining and processing of alum was fully operational again within five years. Alum was valued for its ability to fix dyes by the textile industries; other uses included several applications in leather tanning, and the manufacture of candles and parchment.

Today, Kettleness Point is a dramatic moonscape, offering nesting sites for thousands of seabirds and, to the north, a view of Runswick Bay. The promontory forms part of the Heritage Coast, a sort of linear national park, which aims to preserve undeveloped coastlines with some of the most spectacular scenery along the east coast. Special protection is now given to the 36-mile (57.6km) stretch of superb coastline that lies between Saltburn and Scalby Ness, on the outskirts of Scarborough.

Goldsborough, half a mile (800m) inland, was the site of a 4th-century Roman signal station. The Roman road commonly known as Wade's Causeway was probably built to link the settlement at Malton with the signal stations dotted at regular intervals along the coast. All that remains to be seen on the site are some grassy earthworks, sited 220 yards (200m) from the road linking Kettleness and Goldsborough. Excavations early in the 20th century produced a number of very interesting Roman finds, which suggested that the signal station might have ended its days by being suddenly ransacked. Near by you'll find a modern coastguard station.

The giant, Wade, whose moorland exploits are famous, is, according to legend, buried at Goldsborough. Two standing stones – one by Goldsborough Lane, the other adjacent to the A174 at East Barnby – are known as Wade's Stones and are said to mark the position of his head and feet. The stones are, however, more than half a mile (800m) apart, which would have made him stand out even at a giants' convention.

KETTLENESS POINT

KILDALE MAP REF NZ6009

This little moorland village has a small station on the Esk Valley line between Middlesbrough and Whitby. Completed in 1865, the Esk Valley line had to make 17 river crossings between the stations at Kildale and Grosmont. It is still a valued amenity for locals and visitors.

St Cuthbert's Church is reached via a footbridge over the railway. A hoard of Viking relics, including battleaxes and swords, was found here in 1868 when the church was renovated. These finds show that Kildale was once an ancient settlement, a notion reinforced by earthworks and other finds. A mound, cut into by the railway line, is now the only clue that Kildale once had a motte and bailey castle. This was one of the many strongholds owned by the Percy family, whose name is kept alive by names such as Percy Cross and Percy Rigg, high on the moors.

The Cleveland Way drops down briefly from the moors, to pass through Kildale. If you walk the route going north you will arrive on the breezy heights of Easby Moor where a monument, built in 1827, commemorates the life and exploits of Captain James Cook. From here you can enjoy panoramic views down over Great Ayton, where the young James Cook spent his formative years.

Kildale's rights of way were taken from an old map that marked only three, so there are few of the field paths that typify nearby villages. The road between Kildale and Westerdale offers splendid moorland scenery, and the watersplash over Baysdale Beck is a popular spot for a picnic on a summer's day.

LEALHOLM MAP REF NZ7607

The lovely River Esk runs through the narrow, wooded confines of Crunkly Gill, one of the many ancient gorges carved by Ice Age meltwaters, before flowing through Lealholm's grassy banks. This attractive little village, which sits astride a bend in the river, acts as a magnet for visitors. Lealholm was a favourite place, too, for Canon Atkinson, Danby's vicar, who wrote lyrically about the village in his book, called *Forty Years in a Moorland Parish*, 'Elsewhere you must go in search of beautiful views; here they offer themselves to be looked at.'

The river is spanned by a fine, well proportioned bridge of peach-coloured stone; just a few yards away is a line of ancient stepping stones that seem to have an irresistible attraction for small children. Beyond the bridge is the Board Inn, offering refreshment and another vantage point from which to gaze down over the Esk.

Lealholm boasts no grand buildings of great note, visitors come here largely because the green is common land where they can roam at will and spread a picnic rug. On a sunny summer's day the river bank is a relaxing spot; greedy mallard ducks will eagerly dispose of any leftover sandwiches. Tea rooms and craft shops complete the picture. The National Park Authority has bowed to visitor pressure by providing a car park.

Lealholm can be grouped with other beauty spots, such as Goathland, Hutton-le-Hole and Thornton-le-Dale, as places best avoided on sunny Bank Holidays, unless you love crowds. Apart from that caveat, it's a delightful place.

Around the Cleveland Hills and Esk Dale

This route skirts the Cleveland Hills, passes high cliffs and fishing villages, before exploring the more intimate landscape of the delightful Esk Valley. Staithes, Whitby and the string of villages along the Esk Valley are well worth exploring, and Lealholm, towards the end of the drive, makes an ideal place to stop for a picnic.

Route Directions

The drive starts and ends at Great Ayton, a handsome town where Captain James Cook spent much of his boyhood. Houses overlook the River Leven, and rearing up behind them is Roseberry Topping.

1 Leave Great Ayton along the A173, signposted 'Whitby and Guisborough'. Roseberry Topping is the hill with a 'bite' taken out of its summit due to ironstone mining. Turn right at a roundabout heading

towards Whitby on the A171. Keep straight ahead at the roundabout, on the outskirts of Guisborough, but turn left at the next roundabout, on to the A173, signposted 'Redcar and Saltburn'. Go across another roundabout, almost immediately, and then pass restored Tocketts Mill. Turn left at traffic lights in Skelton (signposted 'Whitby'), soon to go right at a roundabout on the A174, signed 'Brotton & Whitby'. Cross over four more

roundabouts, bear right at the fifth, signposted 'Whitby', and go through Carlin How, to get your first sight of the sea. Follow Whitby signs (A174), down hairpin bends near Skinningrove, where the Cleveland Ironstone Mining Museum can be found.

The mining museum at Skinningrove, located on the site of the Loftus Mine, is based on the collections of enthusiast Tom Leonard who collected mining artifacts.

2 Go through Loftus, still following the A174. Sea views open out as the fishing village of Staithes appears on the horizon. Pass the unsightly bulk of Boulby Potash Mine, and then Staithes.
To visit the delights of the old part of the village leave your car at the top of the village, and explore the village and harbour on foot.

3 Continue on the A174 through rolling farmland past Lythe and its church.
Whitby Abbey can be seen on the horizon as you drop down steeply into Sandsend. Take great care on Lythe Bank; there have been a number of runaways here. After passing Whitby golf club you approach the town itself.

4 At a mini-roundabout, turn right, following signposts for the A171 'Scarborough and Pickering'. Turn right again at a T-junction near a garage. Take the left-hand fork soon after, turn left at another roundabout to arrive at traffic lights. Turn right here, still following the signs for the A171 'Scarborough and Robin Hood's Bay'.
Immediately over the bridge there is a road to your left. This is your route if you want to see the church and abbey at close quarters. Otherwise

your road is to the right, just opposite, and signed, rather unpromisingly, to 'Larpool Lane Industrial Estate'. This unclassified road takes you to Ruswarp village and the River Esk. From here, keep close to the river for most of the way back to Great Ayton.

5 Turn right to cross over Ruswarp's river bridge and adjacent railway line, then turn immediately left on the B1410 to Sleights. Follow the River Esk and then go left at a T-junction on to the A169, signposted 'Pickering'. When you are almost through the village of Sleights, look out for a road on the right, signed 'Grosmont and Egton'.
There are fine views into the delightful Esk Dale before dropping down into Grosmont, where the North Yorkshire Moors Railway connects with the Middlesbrough–Whitby branch line services.

6 Carry on to Egton, where follow the signs left to 'Egton Bridge', turning left again at a T-junction. Turn right just after the church, signposted 'Glaisdale'. Climb steeply to a T-junction; turn left here and negotiate the precipitous 1-in-3 (33%) Limber Hill.
The hill heads down to the ancient stone arch of Beggar's Bridge that once carried

trains of packhorse ponies and over the River Esk.

7 Climb through the straggle of houses in Glaisdale; the signs are now for Lealholm. Keep ahead on the main road, eventually to turn right at a T-junction to descend into Lealholm village.
With its fine arched Beggar's Bridge, stepping stones and grassy riverbanks, this is one of the prettiest villages along the Esk Valley.

8 Cross the bridge over the River Esk, and then turn left immediately, signposted 'Danby'. Pass graceful Duck Bridge and the National Park's Moors Centre, where it's worth stopping if you have time, but otherwise bear left to Danby village. Keep ahead at the crossroads, signposted 'Castleton'. In Castleton village, turn right halfway up the hill, signed 'Guisborough'. Cross the River Esk once again, to climb up on to lovely open moorland. At the first junction by the White Cross base go left on a road signed 'Commondale and Stokesley'. Pass through Commondale, as fine moorland views open up. Continue through Kildale and then take two right turns following the signposts back to 'Great Ayton' and the start of the tour.

ROSEBERRY TOPPING

MAP REF NZ5813

Roseberry Topping, which lies just to the north of Great Ayton, is Cleveland's very own 'Matterhorn'. Its height, just 1,056 feet (322m), hardly qualifies it as a major peak, yet it is a prominent landmark for miles around, standing aloof from the surrounding Cleveland Hills.

To see Roseberry Topping as nature intended, as an almost symmetrical cone, you will have to look at old prints. As soon as its mineral wealth was realised, it was exploited for its alum, iron-ore, jet and roadstone. So heavily was it mined and quarried that a great chunk of the hill fell away in a landslip, making the residents of the nearby village of Newton under Roseberry fear for their lives.

This landslip created the distinctive profile we see today. Climb to the top, and to the northwest is the industrial heartland of Middlesbrough, its urban sprawl creeping inexorably outwards; to the south are views across the moors.

Roseberry Topping's prominence has made it an important landmark for more than a millennia. There is some evidence that it was even an object of veneration. 'Roseberry' is a corruption of the old Viking name, 'Othenesberg' (Odin's Hill), indicating it was probably sacred to the Danish god of creation. 'Topping', also of Scandinavian origin, means a peak. Several 17th-century references have it as 'Osbury Toppyne', at a time when it was one of the many beacon hills on which fires were built – to be set alight if the Spanish Armada were sighted at sea.

RUNSWICK BAY   MAP REF NZ8016

A long arc of sandy beach extends south from the houses of Runswick, to form one of the loveliest bays on the Yorkshire coast. There is plenty of shelter from blustery winds and high seas; over the centuries many a ship's captain has been relieved to find safe harbour here.

The cliffs that protect the bay take a battering each winter; whole chunks can disappear in a storm. Since medieval times the coastline continues to change dramatically, with villages creeping ever closer to the shore, and many coastal villages sliding into the sea. You only have to look at old maps to realise that the 'lost' villages of Yorkshire's coast can be counted in scores.

The village of Runswick fell into the sea in 1682. Fortunately no lives were lost as all the villagers were evacuated in time. Today, Runswick comprises a pleasing collection of small red-roofed cottages, clinging limpet-like to the cliff and connected by a series of steps and alleyways. The sheltering bay, good soil and southerly aspect make Runswick a suntrap; in spring and summer the little terraced gardens make a pretty scene. The attractive whitewashed house on the headland was the coastguard's cottage.

A few fishing cobles are still lined up above the high watermark, though today your neighbour is more likely to be a holiday-maker than a fisherman. The lifeboat is always at the ready, however; ships can still be caught out by sudden changes in the weather. In 1901 a storm blew up while most of the fishing boats were at sea. The village women launched the lifeboat and saved many lives.

Roseberry Topping and Captain Cook Country

Climb Roseberry Topping, once mined for ironstone, for views of the countryside. After the descent from the summit, and the climb again to the woodland, the track descends over Great Ayton Moor. Ahead, the Captain Cook Monument, a stone obelisk 52ft (15.5m) high, dominates the view. The great explorer was born in 1728 within sight of Roseberry Topping at Marton (then a village, but now a suburb of Middlesbrough) and went to school at nearby Great Ayton. Just after you have gone through the gate after Point 5, the dips and hollows in the ground to the left are the remains of an ironstone mine, Ayton Banks. Further on the route you'll pass by Gribdale Terrace, a row of cottages built to house the iron miners and their families.

Route Directions

1 Take the rough lane beside the car park in the direction of Roseberry Topping. The path goes through a gateway then rises to a second gate at the beginning of the woodland.

2 Go through the gate into National Trust land and turn left. There is a well-worn path to the summit, with several variations to the route. Some paths are easier than others but whichever you take, it is a stiff climb to the trig point on the top of the hill.

3 From the summit, take the Cleveland Way path on the opposite side from the ascent, going down a track that rises through a gate to the corner of woodland. Go through another gate and turn right alongside the wood.

4 Follow this track as it follows the edge of the wood. It passes through another gate and goes past a second area of wood, descending the hillside to reach a road.

5 Turn right, cross the cattle grid and bear left past a bench to reach a gate. Turn right to go over a stile, down the field, over another stile and out into a lane. Walk past the cottages to reach a road, where you go straight ahead.

6 At a crossroads go right, down Aireyholme Lane. Follow the lane as it winds past houses, then take a signed footpath left through woodland. After 0.5 miles (800m) go right up a path ascending through the woods, turning left at a crossing path and continuing along the edge of the woodland. Continue bearing right to reach a track to farm buildings, which goes left then right to a gate.

7 Walk across two fields to reach a stile, then continue uphill to the tower. Beyond it, take a grassy path left down a gully, to reach a gate into woodland. Follow the path downhill, walking through the woods to return to the gate at the top of the lane, leading back to the car park.

Route facts

DISTANCE/TIME 5.5 miles (9km) 2h30

MAP OS Explorer OL26 North York Moors – Western

START Car park at Newton under Roseberry, grid ref: NZ 570128

TRACKS Hillside climb, then tracks and field paths, 3 stiles

GETTING TO THE START From Middlesborough, take the A272 towards Stokesley, take a left turn on the B1292 and follow signs to Newton under Roseberry.

THE PUB The Royal Oak Hotel, Great Ayton. Tel: 01642 724047

❶ It is a stiff climb to the top of the hill. Please note that Roseberry Topping is in danger from erosion due to the high number of visitors it attracts each year. You may find that some parts are cordoned off, and access is limited to other areas. Visitors can help conserve the area by ensuring that they stay on the tracks and obey any warning signs.

SANDSEND MAP REF NZ6812

The approach to the lovely Sandsend along the A174 is steeply downhill from Lythe; views open up of a long sandy beach and, in the distance, Whitby Abbey dominates the horizon. Here is a place name that, for once, doesn't require interpretation. Sandsend marks the northern end of a sandy beach, one of the best on Yorkshire's coast, stretching down as far as Whitby harbour.

The village has been an industrious hive of activity for centuries; the Romans had a cement works here. More recently the bare outcrop of Sandsend Ness was mined for alum and it is still bare today, because of the heaps of mining waste. Remarkably, these mines were worked steadily for 250 years. When Yorkshire's coastal area had its railway, Sandsend was overlooked by a long viaduct, raised high above the red-tiled rooftops on tall pillars. Both the railway and the viaduct disappeared in the 1960s: more's the pity, many may think.

Today, Sandsend is a more peaceful spot, sheltered from the from the rough battering of north winds and fiercesome seas by Sandsend Ness. Mickleby Beck and East Row Beck reach to the sea at Sandsend a mere 97 feet (30m) apart; instead of staring out to sea most of the cottages are neatly clustered either side of their banks. Several paths accompany both of these valleys into lovely Mulgrave Woods, which you'll find is a traditional broadleaved woodland.

On the narrow ridge between these valleys is Mulgrave Castle, which is a splendid Georgian pile. Guests at the castle included William Wordsworth and

■ Visit

LEWIS CARROLL

It was while strolling along the fine, sandy beach at Sandsend that Lewis Carroll first had the idea for his surreal poem about the Walrus and the Carpenter. If you fancy it, you can follow in his footsteps; at low tide it is a lovely walk of about 2.5 miles (4km) along the beach to Whitby.

Charles Dickens; both wrote glowingly about the fine views to be ejoyed from here. In the grounds are the evocative, ivy-clad ruins of a much earlier castle, dating from the 13th century.

STAITHES MAP REF NZ7818

It is easy to miss the Staithes turning off the main A174 coast road. Nor is the first sight of the village very promising. You have to drive half a mile (800m), park in the pay-and-display car park and proceed on foot if you want to see why Staithes is so special.

This perfectly preserved Yorkshire fishing villages is divided into two by Cowbar Beck and the steep-sided gorge through which it runs. For centuries the people of Staithes have had to cope with the twin problems of an inhospitable site and the ravages of the North Sea. They have made their living from the sea, while always taking care to respect its awesome power.

The Staithes we see today is a village that would be immediately familiar to the young James Cook, who spent an impatient 18 months working at the counter of a draper's shop in the village before realising his ambition to go to sea. The whitewashed houses, pantiled roofs, fishing cobles and lobster pots would make him feel at home.

It may seem that time has stood still here, but the battering from the sea has been relentless. Despite the shelter given by its steep cliffs, Staithes has lost many buildings to its stormy seas. The little draper's shop was washed away; a house near the Cod and Lobster pub bears a commemorative plaque but has been rebuilt since James Cook lived and worked here. The pub itself backs on to the harbour wall and has suffered more than its fair share of storm damage, having been rebuilt three times – the last occasion being as recently as 1953.

■ Activity

VIEWPOINTS ABOVE STAITHES
A walk of less than an hour from the village of Staithes will offer a variety of viewpoints, looking down on the random patchwork of red-tiled roofs from the cliff tops – known as Cowbar Nab and Old Nab – on either side of the gorge, connected by the arch of a footbridge.

■ Insight

A MAJOR FISHING PORT
Sleepy Staithes has known busier days. During the first half of the 19th century as many as 300 men went to sea in the distinctive fishing cobles, to net mostly cod, haddock and mackerel. These small craft, with a crew of three, were often accompanied by larger yawls. Fish were moved from the cobles into larger vessels for easier transport back to harbour. Fish was dispatched from Staithes all over the country; packhorses were maintained to do nothing more than to carry some of each day's catch to the market at York.

On a sunny summer's day it is hard to imagine such destruction. You would have to make your visit in winter, when a strong northeasterly gale is blowing, and the waves are hammering against the harbour wall, to understand why the people of Staithes have earned a reputation for self-reliance. To have maintained a viable community here, despite the drawbacks, is remarkable.

Fishing has long provided a living, albeit a precarious one, for the men of Staithes. The little harbour, and the mouth of Cowbar Beck, are still full of the traditional fishing cobles – whose slightly upturned prows betray their Nordic origins. But today they go to sea mainly for crabs and lobsters; you can buy them freshly caught in the village.

Painters and photographers are attracted in droves to the village. There are echoes of some of the picturesque fishing villages of Cornwall, but few communities in the country can boast a more extraordinary setting than Staithes. The village used to have a railway station; both station and line are gone, leaving just the trackbed and the stanchions of the old viaduct over the gorge as reminders of the scenic line from Saltburn to Scarborough.

To the north of Staithes are Boulby Cliffs. At more than 650 feet (200m) they are the highest, if not the most dramatic, on England's east coast and offer excellent views. Close by is the Boulby Potash Mine, the deepest mine in Europe. The extent of the mining operation here can be gauged by the fact that tunnels extend almost 3 miles (4.8km) out under the sea.

WHITBY MAP REF NZ8910

Those who take a leisurely stroll along the pleasant harbour front may be forgiven for thinking of Whitby as just another resort devoted to the arcane delights of bingo, amusement arcades, candyfloss and 'Kiss Me Quick' hats. But Whitby has a great deal more to offer, enough to keep the most demanding visitor interested for some time. For it has a long, illustrious and genuine history as one of the country's most important seaports, and the town can claim associations with a remarkable variety of historical figures.

Whitby's setting itself is dramatic, with houses clinging on to the steep slopes on either side of the River Esk. A good overview of the town can be enjoyed from the elevated bridge that now carries through traffic on the A171 at a convenient distance from the town's narrow streets. From this vantage point you can see the Esk broaden into a large marina full of yachts. Beyond the swing bridge is the harbour, overlooked spectacularly on the southern flank by St Mary's Church and the ruined abbey – a landmark for miles around.

The scene is always one of bustle and activity. Whitby has thrived when other fishing towns and villages have declined, and new building projects emphasise that the town is looking to the future as well as the past.

Whitby has always gazed out to sea. For centuries the town was isolated from the rest of the county by poor roads and the wild expanse of moorland that surround it on three sides. Yet by the 18th century it had risen to the status of

◼ Insight

FRANK MEADOW SUTCLIFFE

Photographer Frank Meadow Sutcliffe's bread-and-butter work was portraiture. But his passion was Whitby itself. He used a huge and cumbersome camera, which precluded any modern notion of candid photography, to photograph the town. He stage-managed his compositions (even paying some of his subjects to ensure co-operation) to produce lustrous images of gnarled old fishermen, street traders and grubby street urchins – with the tall-masted sailing ships and Whitby harbour as picturesque backdrops.It isn't merely the patina of age that makes Sutcliffe's pictures so beguiling. All the characters he photographed may be long gone, but many of the locations can still be seen today. Despite the cars, the cafés and the candyfloss, there is a continuing thread that links the Whitby of today to the Whitby that Sutcliffe knew so well. At the Sutcliffe Gallery you can find framed prints of his evocative photographs, all taken from the original negatives.

a major port, with shipbuilding, fishing and whaling contributing to a maritime prosperity that lasted until well into the early years of the 20th century. The fine Georgian houses at the west end of the town, built by wealthy shipbuilders and fleet owners, attest to this success.

Elsewhere, more traditional cottages, whitewashed and with red-tiled roofs housed the fishermen. Space was at a premium, so their houses were built in close proximity, mostly up the steep inclines on the eastern side of the Esk. They are linked by ginnels and steps, which beg to be explored. Be sure to leave your car in one of the long-stay car

■ Insight

WHITBY JET

Used to make jewellery since the Bronze Age, Whitby jet was popularised by Queen Victoria, who wore it during her many years of mourning for Prince Albert. Jet is fossilised wood, which turns from its natural brown colour to the deepest black ('jet-black', as we say) once it is polished, and Whitby proved a particularly fruitful site. This craft trade expanded as women took the royal lead and took to wearing jet ornaments. But their tastes were too fickle for the business to last, and by the time of Victoria's death the demand for Whitby jet was much reduced. Today you can find original pieces of jewellery displayed in Whitby's Pannett Park Museum, and for sale in the town's antiques shops. Some new jet jewellery is being made too.

parks near the marina; Whitby's narrow streets were definitely not built with motor traffic in mind.

The town's large harbour is still at the heart of the town, though today there are more pleasure craft passing the breakwaters than fishing cobles. Whitby traditionally offered the only safe harbour between the rivers Tyne and Humber. The North Yorkshire coast is notoriously prone to storms, and many ships have been wrecked, unable to find sanctuary in time.

The town was prosperous during the 17th and 18th centuries with the mining and refining of alum – a vital ingredient in the dyeing of wool. Coal was brought here to fire the cauldrons that separated alum from rock, and stone was needed for building; this increase in trade

required the building of a better harbour. In 1753 a company was set up in the town to undertake whaling expeditions, using the sturdy ships already being built here. The ships spent many weeks at sea in the distant, inhospitable waters of the Arctic. The trade was lucrative for those who survived; some ships, sadly, never returned. Records reveal that almost 3,000 whales were brought back to Whitby up to 1833. Seals, walruses and polar bears also featured in these hauls, and even unicorns, if the records are to be believed. They were more likely to have been narwhals, whose single 'horn' probably started the unicorn myth in the first place.

The whale blubber was rendered down on the quayside to make oil; the stench, by all accounts, was vile. Even the streetlamps of the town were lit with gas refined from whale oil. An arch formed from the jawbone of a whale looks down upon the harbour today.

Smaller boats sailed out of Whitby to net herring, and the fish market was one of the busiest. The men still fish, but on a much reduced scale; many of the boats that slip anchor today are carrying sea anglers and other visitors.

The town has a special place in ecclesiastical history. In the year AD 655 King Oswy of Northumbria celebrated a heady victory in battle by promising his daughter as a bride of Christ. He founded a monastery on Whitby's eastern cliff, overlooking the town, much where the later abbey's ruins still stand today. The first abbess was Hilda, who presided over a community of nuns and monks. Her goodness and piety passed into legend, and she was recognised as a saint. II AD 664 the Synod of Whitby convened in the town to decide whether Northumbria should follow the Catholic or Celtic Christianity. In the event the Catholic Church triumphed.

The most notable member of this community was a monk, Caedmon, who is also known as the 'Father of English poetry'. A shy man, he preferred to keep his own company as a cowherd instead of singing with the choir. Caedmon had a dream in which an angel asked him to sing. When he awoke, he found that he was possessed of a beautiful voice. His poem, called *The Song of Creation*, is the earliest known poem written in English. A sandstone cross, which stands by St Mary's Church commemorates the lifes of Caedmon and carved panels illustrate some of the incidents in his life.

St Hilda's original abbey was destroyed by Viking raiders. The abbey that replaced it was begun in the 11th century and was rebuilt on several occasions, notably in the 13th and 14th centuries; this is what we can see today, starkly silhouetted against the sky. This building, too, suffered damage, when in 1914 two German battleships shelled the town and inadvertently hit the west front of Whitby Abbey.

Sharing the abbey's windswept site is St Mary's Church. It was built to cater for the spiritual needs of the village that grew up around the abbey. St Mary's still serves the congregations, although its parishioners have to tackle the famous 199 steps up to the church. Parts of the building date back to the 12th century; fortunately the fabric of the church suffered none of the indignities meted out to the abbey. Make sure to take a look inside St Mary's; the interior was fitted out during the 18th century with wooden galleries, high-sided box-pews and a splendid three-decker pulpit. The effect is quite startling, with a distinctly nautical feeling as the craftsmen were more accustomed to fitting out ships.

At the bottom of Church Steps is the oldest part of town. Little fishermen's cottages huddle together as if to keep out the bitter weather. Narrow alleyways lead off from the tiny market square, and if those 199 steps have taken their toll enjoy a drink in one of the harbour-side pubs and watch the fishing boats and pleasure craft.

On Grape Lane, by the harbour, you will find the home of ship owner and Quaker, Captain John Walker, to whom the young James Cook was apprenticed in 1746, before enlisting in the Royal Navy. Today the building houses the Captain Cook Memorial Museum, with fascinating room sets and interesting exhibits about his life.

■ Insight

DRACULA

Few graveyards enjoy a more panoramic view than the one surrounding St Mary's Church. But if the wind is whipping around the gravestones, and the full moon is shrouded by clouds, it can have a rather more menacing atmosphere. Bram Stoker realised its potential and avid readers of his horror novel, *Dracula*, will recognise some of the settings from Whitby. Look out for the skull and crossbones gravestones near the topmost gate. These are said to have inspired the novel.

■ TOURIST INFORMATION CENTRES

Danby
The Moors Centre.
Tel: 01287 660654

Great Ayton
High Green Car Park.
Tel: 01642 722835 (Seasonal).

Guisborough
Priory Grounds, Church Street. Tel: 01287 633801

Whitby
Langborne Road.
Tel: 01723 383636

■ PLACES OF INTEREST

There will be an admission charge at the places of interest unless otherwise stated.

Captain Cook and Staithes Heritage Centre
High Street, Staithes.
Tel: 01947 841454

Captain Cook Memorial Museum
Grape Lane, Whitby.
Tel: 01947 601900; www.cookmuseumwhitby.co.uk

Captain Cook Schoolroom Museum
Great Ayton.
Tel: 01642 724296;
www.captaincookschoolroommuseum.co.uk

The Dracula Experience
9 Marine Parade,
Whitby.
Tel: 01947 601923

Gisborough Priory
Guisborough.
Tel: 01287 633801

Lifeboat Museum
Pier Road, Whitby.
Tel: 01947 602001

The Moors Centre
Lodge Lane, Danby.
Tel: 01439 772737 or 01287 660792;
www.nationalparks.gov.uk/nym_core
Free.

Tocketts Watermill
On A173, 1 mile (1.6km) east of Guisborough.

Tom Leonard Mining Museum
Skinningrove.
Tel: 01287 642877;
www.ironstonemuseum.co.uk

Victorian Jet Works
123B Church Street, Whitby.
Tel: 01947 821530;
www.whitbyjet.net
Shop free; fee for museum.

Whitby Abbey
East Cliff, Whitby.
Tel: 01947 603568

Whitby Museum and Art Gallery
Pannett Park, Whitby.
Tel: 01947 602908

■ SHOPPING

Guisborough
Open-air market,
Thu and Sat.

Whitby
Open-air market,
Tue and Sat.

LOCAL SPECIALITIES

Ceramics, Sculpture and Jewellery
Montage Studio Gallery,
12 Church Street, Castleton.
Tel: 01287 660159

Enamel
The Enamel Gallery,
128 Church Street, Whitby.
Tel: 01947 606216

Glass
Whitby Glass Studios,
9 Sandgate, Whitby.
Tel: 01947 603553;
www.whitbyglass.com

Paintings and Prints
John Freeman Studios,
9 Market Place, Whitby.
Tel: 01947 602799;
www.johnfreemanstudio.co.uk

Grosmont Gallery
Grosmont.
Tel: 01947 895007;
www.grosmontgallery.com

Whitby Jet
Watsons Jet Workshop,
Church Street, Whitby.
Tel: 01947 605320

Whitby Jet Heritage Centre,
Church Street, Whitby.
Tel: 01947 821530;
www.whitbyjet.net
Shop free; fee for workshop.

■ PERFORMING ARTS

Glaisdale
Esk Valley Summer Theatre (seasonal).
Tel: 01947 897587

Whitby Pavilion Theatre
West Cliff, Whitby.
Tel: 01947 604855 or 820625;
www.whitbypavilion.co.uk

■ SPORTS & ACTIVITIES
ANGLING
Sea
Staithes & Whitby
Enquire at the harbour,
or contact the local TIC.
Fly
River Esk
Information on licences and
permits from main post
offices. Fishing locations
from the Environment
Agency, Rivers House,
21 Park Square South, Leeds.
Tel: 0113 2440191
Scaling Dam Reservoir
Fishing lodge:
Tel: 01287 640540
BEACHES
Runswick Bay has a sandy
beach with easy access; a
sandy beach stretches from
Whitby to Sandsend with car
parks and access points.
BOAT TRIPS
Whitby
Trips round the bay leave
from the West Pier.
CYCLE HIRE
Hawsker (Whitby to
Scarborough rail trail)
Trailways Cycle Hire,
The Old Railway Station,
Hawsker, near Whitby.
Tel: 01947 820207;
www.trailways.info

HORSE RIDING
Lealholm
Hollin Hall Riding Centre,
Great Fryup Dale.
Tel: 01947 897470;
www.hollinequest.co.uk
Borrowby
Borrowby Equestrian Centre,
High Farm, Borrowby.
Tel: 01947 840134;
www.borrowbyequestriancent
re.co.uk
LONG-DISTANCE FOOTPATHS AND TRAILS
The Cleveland Way
A 110-mile (176km) walk
from Helmsley to Filey Brigg.
www.clevelandway.gov.uk
The Esk Valley Walk
Begins at Castleton and
follows the River Esk to
Whitby.
WATER SPORTS
Scaling Dam Reservoir
Sailing, windsurfing.
Tel: 01287 640214

■ ANNUAL EVENTS & CUSTOMS
Castleton
Castleton Show, Sep.
Danby
Agricultural Show,
mid-Aug.
Egton
Egton Show, late Aug.
Egton Bridge
Gooseberry Show,
early Aug.
Kildale
Kildale Show, early Sep.

Lealholm
Lealholm Show, early Sep.
Whitby
Planting of the Penny Hedge,
Ascension Eve, May.
Morris Dance Festival, Jun.
Blessing of Boats, mid-Jul.
Whitby Angling Festival, Jul.
Whitby Folk Festival, Aug.
Whitby Regatta, mid-Aug.

Tea Rooms

Danby

**Stonehouse Bakery &
Tea Shop,
3 Briar Hill Avenue, Danby,
YO21 2LZ. Tel: 01287 660006**
In the centre of Danby, this
traditional bakery produces
fabulous bread, including
sun-dried tomato and olive
breads and ciabatta. They are
used to make the range of
delicious sandwiches that
available in the adjoining tea
shop. Cakes, too, come from
the bakery's ovens, and their
scones are perfect with jam
and cream in a traditional
cream tea.

Guisborough

**Macdonald Gisborough Hall,
Whitby Lane, Guisborough,
TS14 6PT. Tel: 0870 400 8191
www.macdonaldhotels.co.uk
/gisborough**
For a taste of luxury, in
elegant surroundings, treat
yourself at Gisborough Hall.
As well as the traditional
scones with jam and cream,
there's the Gisborough Hall
Tea, with smoked salmon
and ham finger sandwiches,
chocolate brownies and
boiled fruit cake, as well as
the scones, or the Yorkshire
Tea, where your scones and
fruitcake are accompanied by
Wensleydale cheese. Tea is
served from midday to 6pm.

Lealholm

**Beck View Tea Room,
Lealholm, YO21 2AQ.
Tel: 01947 897310**
There are tables inside the
cosy tea room and outside
on the beck's bank. As well
as good-value cream teas,
regular visitors enjoy a good
variety of home-made cakes,
including the particularly
scrumptious nut slice.

Whitby

**Elizabeth Botham & Sons
35/39 Skinner Street, Whitby,
YO21 3AH. Tel: 01947 602823
www.botham.co.uk**
The tradition of fine baking,
begun in 1865, is still going
strong in this superior first
floor café on Whitby's West
Cliff. Your problem will be
what to choose – gingerbread
with Wensleydale cheese,
lemon buns, Yorkshire tea
brack loaf, the cream tea, or
the salads, the sandwiches
or baked potatoes.

Pubs

Danby

**Duke of Wellington Inn
Danby, YO21 2LY.
Tel: 01287 660351;
www. danby-
dukeofwellington.co.uk**
An attractive inn, in the
scattered village of Danby
with wide views of the village
in its moorland setting.
Inside, the décor is warm,
welcoming and traditional,
with local beers and a good
selection of whiskies. The
evening menu tends to be
more adventurous than the
lunchtime offerings.

Egton

**The Wheatsheaf Inn,
Egton, YO21 1TZ.
Tel: 01947 895271**
There's a plentiful supply
of Yorkshire ales in the
Wheatsheaf, including Black
Sheep from Masham. The
pub's exterior is unassuming,
but inside, the main bar has
low beams, dark walls and
comfortable settles. There is
much good pub food on offer,
using local fish and other
produce – the fish stew is
recommended.

Great Ayton

**The Royal Oak Hotel
125 High Street, Great Ayton,
TS9 6BW. Tel: 01642 722361
www.royaloak-hotel.co.uk**
Located in the heart of the
tranquil village of Great
Ayton, you'll find the Royal
Oak to be a traditional,
relaxed pub. The beamed bar
provides good local beer and
hearty bar snacks, while the
restaurant serves simple,
robust and well-cooked food
with a range of puddings, so
leave room for one.

Western Moors

AMPLEFORTH ■ BILSDALE ■ BRANSDALE

CHRISTIAN CROSSES & MONKS ■ CLEVELAND WAY ■ COXWOLD

HAWNBY ■ WALK 2 ■ HELMSLEY ■ KILBURN ■ OSMOTHERLEY

WALK 3 ■ CAR TOUR 2 ■ OSWALDKIRK ■ RIEVAULX ABBEY

STOKESLEY ■ SUTTON BANK ■ CYCLE RIDE 1 ■ WALK 4

The Western Moors include Helmsley, a handsome little market town and the administrative centre of the National Park. Near by you'll find the ruins of Rievaulx and Byland abbeys and the White Horse of Kilburn. The rolling Hambleton Hills and the bleaker Cleveland Hills provide a landscape of heather moorland and pastoral dales, dotted with farmhouses and villages of red-tiled stone houses.

3 Walk start point

1 Cycle start point

2 Tour start point

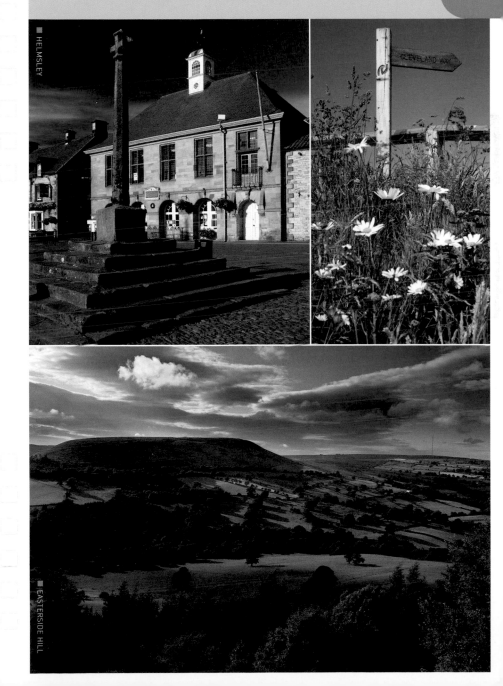

HELMSLEY

CLEVELAND WAY

EASTERSIDE HILL

Unmissable attractions

There's no lack of things to enjoy here and Helmsley is a good base from which to explore the Western Moors...take a picnic to Chop Gate for fine views...walk the drove road called Westside Track near Cockayne...stroll on Rievaulx Terrace and view the fine abbey below...walk northwards from the car park at Sutton Bank along part of (or all) of the Cleveland Way for magnificent views...see the craftsmen carvers hard at work at the Mouseman Visitor Centre in Kilburn...follow the Mosaic Trail from Boltby...explore the ruins of Helmsley Castle...contemplate a monk's life in a cell at Mount Grace Priory...catch a concert in a remote country church during the Ryedale Festival...see Coxwold's octagonal church tower from the gardens of Shandy Hall.

1

2

1 Rievaulx Abbey
The atmospheric and evocative ruins of 13th-century Rievaulx Abbey, one of the great monastic houses of the north, are set in the tranquil wooded valley of the River Rye.

2 Hemlsley Castle
Little remains of Helmsley Castle's great East Tower, built in the 12th century by Robert de Roos. The castle was destroyed by Parliamentarians after a three-month siege in 1644; the story is told in the visitor centre.

3 Sutton Bank
The wonderful views from the vantage point of Sutton Bank, on the edge of the Hambleton Hills, take in the prominent landmark of Roulston Scar, wooded Hood Hill and the Vale of York.

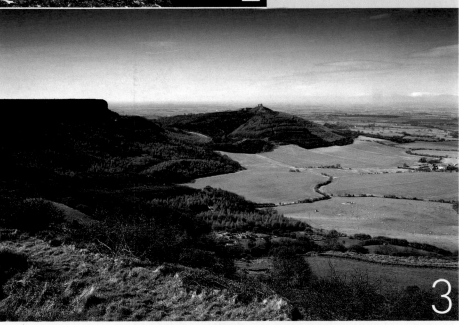

3

AMPLEFORTH MAP REF SE5878

Best known for its boys' public school and Benedictine monastery, Ampleforth is a linear village of handsome houses overlooking the Howardian Hills.

French monks, fleeing persecution in their homeland in 1793 during the course of the French Revolution, found spiritual sanctuary in England and patronage from the prominent Fairfax family, settling at Ampleforth in 1802. As theirs had been a teaching order, they built a school within the monastery. The oldest surviving school buildings date from 1861, while the monastery dates from 1894–98. But both establishments have been extended almost continuously up to the present day.

Just after the end of World War I, headmaster Father Paul Nevill, who was also the parish priest, commissioned Robert Thompson of Kilburn to make a wooden cross for the churchyard in the village. Father Nevill was so impressed by the woodcarver's craftsmanship that Thompson was asked to make furniture for the school. The library remains one of Robert Thompson's most ambitious commissions. The present abbey church is a new addition, built between 1922 and 1961 to a design by Sir Giles Gilbert Scott; it too contains several very fine examples of woodwork and carvings by Robert Thompson.

Just southeast of Ampleforth is Gilling East, which has a 14th-century fortified tower house. Since early in the 20th century the building has been owned by Ampleforth College, and used as the college's preparatory school.

■ Visit

PICNIC SITES

Five miles (8km) north of Helmsley on the B1257, just before you enter Bilsdale, is Newgate Bank, a fine vantage point with a picnic site, from where you can enjoy views of Bilsdale and the Hambleton Hills. A footpath returns to Helmsley via Riccal Bank. At the northern end of Bilsdale is the village of Chop Gate, which also has a picnic site and a car park.

■ Visit

BRIDESTONES

On top of Hasty Bank, the northern escarpment of the Cleveland Hills, are the Wainstones, the largest outcrop of rocks in the National Park, and a favourite with climbers. Another set of rocks can be found on Nab End Moor, in Bilsdale. These are just one of a number of rock formations on the moors that are known as the Bridestones. Others, the remains of ancient stone circles, can be found near Grosmont. The best-known Bridestones are in the hands of the National Trust on Bridestones Moor, and are most easily approached from the Dalby Forest Drive. Weathered into strange shapes, these ricks make a surreal moorland landmark.

BILSDALE

The long valley of Bilsdale extends all the way along the B1257, from Helmsley in the south towards Stokesley in the north. The broad valley is farmed up to the moorland tops, as it was centuries ago by the monks of Rievaulx Abbey. The monastic connection is recalled by names such as Crossholme and Low Crosses Farm. Scattered farmsteads punctuate the valley, but today the only village is tiny Chop Gate. Pronounce it 'Chop Yat' to sound like a local.

The River Seph is ever-present in the valley bottom; the B1257 accompanies it almost from its source to where it joins the River Rye to the north of Rievaulx. On the roadside about 8 miles (12.8km) north of Helmsley is the Sun Inn. Just yards away from the pub is a much earlier thatched building, of cruck-frame construction, that dates back to the 16th century. This was the original Sun Inn – also known as Spout House – which dispensed ale from first receiving its licence in 1714 until 1914.

When the licence transferred to the new Sun Inn, the older building fell into disrepair. The National Park Authority rescued and renovated this delightful example of vernacular architecture. Now it is considered to be the finest example of a cruck-framed house in the National Park (not counting those in Ryedale Folk Museum) and one of the oldest. Visitors can take a look inside.

The interior has been restored to how it might have looked more than three centuries ago. A witch post still stands near the inglenook fireplace, to ward off the 'evil eye'. Up narrow stairs are tiny rooms, open to the thatch and fitted out with wooden box beds. Downstairs are the diminutive bar and snugs of the original pub layout, and the beer cellar.

BRANSDALE

The unspoiled valley of Bransdale drives deep into the moors, but most visitors pass it by. Motorists leaving Helmsley along the A170 towards Kirkbymoorside should look out on the left for a signpost to Carlton (and Helmsley Youth Hostel). The road loops around Bransdale and

■ Visit

THE GILLAMOOR SUNDIAL

Gillamoor boasts a sundial of novel design in front of Dial House Farm; it was erected by public subscription in 1800. A central column is mounted on top of a stepped base. On top is a stone globe mounted on an inscribed cube, with a dial face on four of its sides.

■ Activity

A CYCLE TOUR THROUGH BRANSDALE

The unclassified road which leaves the A170 at Helmsley and curves round in a loop through Bransdale before rejoining the A170 again at Kirkbymoorside is an ideal route for cyclists. Passing through the villages of Carlton, Cockayne and Gillamoor, the 12-mile (19km) tour offers wonderful moorland views with lonely farms and tumbling streams.

then returns to the A170 about 5 miles (8km) further east at Kirkbymoorside. This is a delightful drive.

Beyond the houses that comprises the village of Carlton, the views open up dramatically. To the left is unenclosed heather moorland; to the right the valley bottom is divided up by neat drystone walls either side of Hodge Beck. This pattern is punctuated by a handful of scattered farmsteads. The moors, with barely a tree to be seen, echo to the evocative calls of the curlew, red grouse and lapwing; sheep graze the grassy verges and wander idly across the road. Unenclosed for most of the way, the road heads north; look out on the left for examples of inscribed milestones.

The Church of St Nicholas sits on a hillock overlooking the valley. Though dating only from 1886, the building replaces a much earlier church. It is a typical moorland church, tiny and rather undemonstrative, but with a real sense of spirituality that grander churches so often lack. Inside, the barrelled roof is worth a look.

Flour was ground for centuries at Bransdale Mill (National Trust, but not open to the public), accessible, on foot only, from either side of the valley head. The present building, dating from 1811, was built by William Strickland and his son, Emmanuel, the vicar of Ingleby Greenhow. Stones inset into the mill walls are inscribed with 'improving' texts in Hebrew, Latin and Greek; evidence of the vicar's classical education.

The road then makes a broad sweep to the right, before continuing the circuit of Bransdale. Here sturdy farmsteads with fanciful names – Cow Sike, Toad Hole and Spout House – gaze down into the bottom of the valley. Before arriving in Kirkbymoorside, you have a chance to visit Gillamoor and Fadmoor, a pair of typical moorland villages barely half a mile (800m) apart.

The houses of both these pretty and unspoilt villages are grouped around their village greens, but Gillamoor has an extra surprise in store for the visitor. St Aidan's Church stands on its own at the end of the village; you are almost upon it before you see that it is sited on the edge of a steep precipice which commands breathtaking views across lower Farndale, the River Dove and on to the purple heather moors beyond.

CHRISTIAN CROSSES & MONKS

The life and landscape of the North York Moors have been shaped by a number of influences, but few have had a longer or more profound effect than the Christian faith. The moorland monasteries may be evocative ruins today, but in days gone by the influence of these communities extended far beyond the silence of their cloisters. For example, by the start of the 16th century about a third of the land within what is now the Peak District National Park was under the direct control of various monasteries.

The monks combined their religious devotions with remarkably successful forays into more secular activities. They may have chosen isolated sites on which to build their communities and churches, but they were not averse to comfort – even luxury. The religious buildings of the moors trace their origins back many centuries. A number of extant churches and abbeys pre-date the Norman invasion. Many more recent edifices are built on the foundations of much earlier buildings. The link with the past is everywhere to be seen.

At the dawning of the 7th century, these moors formed part of the Northumbrian Kingdom of Deira. King Edwin of Northumbria was saved from assassination by the intervention of Lilla, one of his ministers. Edwin is said to have marked Lilla's grave on Fylingdales Moor with a stone cross – the oldest of the famous moorland crosses. In AD 627 Edwin was converted to Christianity by Paulinus, a Roman missionary. The first Christian communities in the area

■ Insight

ANCIENT WAYMARKERS

More than thirty moorland stone crosses still survive today; at one time there were many more. One of their functions was to define the far-flung boundaries of the sheep-grazing moors of the monasteries. But their religious symbolism is obvious, and many a lost and lonely traveller would have had his spirits lifted by the sight of a cross on the horizon. Crosses were often sited along old roads and many doubled as waymarkers. An interesting custom was for well-heeled travellers to leave coins on top of the crosses (many had a recess for this purpose) for the benefit of their needier brethren.

■ Insight

ENTREPRENEURIAL MONKS

The various monastic communities of the North York moors owned outlying farms – known as granges, which were often located many miles from the monasteries. The monks (their numbers augmented by lay brothers) devoted their talents to arable farming, animal husbandry and exploiting the uplands for their mineral wealth. The monks' entrepreneurial skills created international markets for their wares and, in many cases, immense wealth and power for the monasteries.

■ Activity

THE MISSING LINK

An extra section of the Cleveland Way, known as the Missing Link, has been developed to take walkers in a complete loop from Scarborough back to Helmsley. This circular walk is about 180 miles (288km) long, and means that walkers can now start and finish at any convenient point on the route.

covered by this book were in Whitby (at that time known as Streanaeshalch) and Lastingham. In AD 654 St Cedd was given land at Lastingham on which to build a monastery. Just three years later Whitby Abbey was founded by Abbess Hilda, who presided over male and female devotees on this exposed cliff-top site.

Although the monasteries of Whitby and Lastingham were sacked by the Vikings, the seeds of Christianity proved to have been sown in fertile ground. By the end of the 10th century the Danish and Norwegian settlers had mostly been converted to the faith. St Gregory's Minster at Kirkdale is a fascinating pre-Norman church.

It was only after the Norman invasion, however, that the great monastic houses on the moors were founded. Benedictine monks returned to the site of St Hilda's monastery in Whitby and established another five communities in the area. The Cistercian Order was created by French monks. Finding the Benedictine regime too ready to succumb to earthly temptations, they vowed to emphasise once again the virtues of hard work and austerity. In 1131 a band of monks from France crossed the Channel and were endowed with land in Ryedale on which to build a monastery. The monks gave a French twist to the valley's name and called their community Rievaulx.

From small beginnings the Cistercian community prospered. By the time of the third abbot, St Aelred, the number of ordained monks – about 150 – was swelled by more than 600 lay brethren. Outlying farms, known as 'granges', were set up – often at some distance from the mother church. Contemplation and prayer played a great part in the monks' lives, but they worked hard too.

The monks of Rievaulx developed the mining of ironstone that, many centuries on, would help to create the industrial wealth around the Tees and the Tyne. The upland moors provided grazing for huge flocks of sheep. The land (a gift from a local landowner) may have been poor for agriculture, but the monks successfully exploited it as grazing land. Wool from Rievaulx became renowned throughout Europe for its excellence.

The monks cleared forests to provide fuel for the iron furnaces. They drained land, built roads and spanned the River Rye and other rivers with sturdy bridges. They even built a system of canals to facilitate the transport of iron and stone. All this activity was in addition to the huge task, undertaken over a period of 60 years, of building Rievaulx Abbey; the impressive remains of the high church and monastic buildings still lift the spirits of visitors today.

The Carthusian Order was another to have had its origins in France. Mount Grace Priory, near Osmotherley, was founded in 1398, the ruins are believed to be the finest example of Carthusian building in the country.

Franciscan friars, who followed the strict teachings of St Francis, came to Scarborough. Their doctrine of absolute poverty provided a stark contrast to the business-like ethos and prosperity of the Carthusians. The Augustinian Canons built the splendid Gisborough Priory; visitors to the site can see the great arch of the east window that still stands.

Between 1536 and 1540, after his break with Rome, Henry VIII ordered the closure of the abbeys and monasteries, bringing to an end their huge and wide-ranging influence.

CLEVELAND WAY

When it was inaugurated in 1969 the Cleveland Way was only the second national trail in the country – coming just four years after Tom Stephenson's pioneering work in creating the Pennine Way. The name of the walk derives from the Cleveland Hills and is a little ambiguous, since for most of its 110-mile (176km) length it lies inside the North York Moors National Park.

The walk, a roughly horseshoe-shaped route, breaks into two distinct sections. From the starting point at Helmsley, the route meanders through the moorland scenery of the Hambleton and Cleveland Hills. Walkers reach the highest point within the National Park when they traverse Urra Moor. Once the North Sea is sighted, at Saltburn, walkers follow the coastal path down to the finishing point at Filey Brigg. The walk can be divided up into sections that offer a single day's hike, with each section ending at a point where budget accommodation is available.

COXWOLD MAP REF SE5377

Coxwold, about 3 miles (5km) south of Kilburn, has a 15th-century village church, with a distinctive eight-sided tower, overlooking the handsome houses lining the broad main street, which include almshouses dating back to the reign of Charles II.

Fifteenth-century Shandy Hall, lies opposite to the church, and was once the home of Laurence Sterne (1713–68). As a writer Sterne was a relatively late developer, not picking up his quill until the ripe age of 46. The publication of his picaresque novel, *The Life and Opinions of Tristram Shandy, Gentleman*, coincided with his becoming the vicar of Coxwold. Literary success was immediate, and Sterne was able to indulge his taste for high living. He contracted pleurisy and died in 1768. His skull is buried in Coxwold churchyard. Dilapidated Shandy Hall was renovated in the 1960s and filled with manuscripts and first editions and opened to the public.

To the south of Coxwold is Newburgh Priory, which was designed and built as an Augustinian house in 1145. After the Dissolution of Monasteries, Henry VIII rewarded his chaplain, Anthony Bellasis, by giving him the building. He, and the owners who followed him, transformed the priory into a fine country house.

The beautiful setting of Byland Abbey (English Heritage) wasn't the first site chosen by the band of Cistercian monks who came here from France. They had settled briefly near Old Byland, but it was reckoned to be unsuitable because the monks were confused by hearing the bells of nearby Rievaulx Abbey. Finally, in 1177, work began on Byland Abbey. Not as complete now as either Rievaulx or Fountains Abbeys, its church was nevertheless larger than either. The dramatic west façade, with its 26-foot (8m) diameter window, still stands to its full height, and gives an impression of just how huge the nave used to be.

HAWNBY MAP REF SE5489

The remote village of Hawnby is best approached from the south. A long view opens up, with the red-roofed houses of the village appearing to cling to a ledge on the flank of Hawnby Hill. This sunny situation encourages residents to create colourful terraced gardens. To the right are the equally rounded contours of Easterside Hill. The environs of Hawnby comprise one of the loveliest landscapes in the National Park and it is well worth leaving the car and exploring on foot.

Winding roads and tracks offer superb views at every turn. This gently undulating moorland landscape left an impression on John Wesley, the founder of Methodist Church, who came here to preach in 1757: 'I rode through one of the pleasantest parts of England to Hawnby'. Wesley's inspirational sermons in Hawnby gained it a reputation as a stronghold of Methodism.

He had come from Osmotherley, across the expanse of Snilesworth Moor, so it would have been a relief to arrive in the sheltered, wooded valley of the River Rye. The road between Hawnby and Osmotherley has a rather better surface than in Wesley's day, but it still twists and turns through beautiful countryside.

The little Church of All Saints, in a riverside setting near the bridge, has features which date to the 12th century. Beyond the church is Arden Hall (not open), almost hidden in the woods. It was built on the site of a 12th-century Benedictine nunnery, the hall is the seat of the Earls of Mexborough. Mary, Queen of Scots, stayed here on her long road to the executioner's axe.

A Loop from Swainby to Whorlton

From the once-industrial villge of Swainby, this walks takes in fine views from the northern edge of the North York Moors plateau. The route then passes through Whorlton village, deserted since it was devastated by the plague in the 14th century.

Route Directions

1 With the church on your left, take the street to the right of the stream. Continue past a sign 'Unsuitable for Coaches' and head uphill. As the road bends to the right, follow the bridleway sign to Scugdale, up the track ahead.

2 Go through two gates, turning left after the second into the woods to join the waymarks for the Cleveland

Way National Trail. Walk through the woodland, turning left, at an opening, down to a stile. The footpath goes downhill across the fields to another gate. Cross the stream on the footbridge then turn left along a lane, with another footbridge, over Scugdale Beck.

3 Follow the lane past Hollin Hill Farm to a T-junction with telephone and post boxes. Cross the lane and go through a Cleveland Way signed gate. Walk up the path beside woodland to a gate (there's valley views from this ridge).

4 The path turns right to a gate and goes on to a paved track in the wood. Go straight ahead at a crossing track to another gate, and continue to follow the paved path on to the heather moorland. After the first summit, the path descends beyond a cairn into a dip. After the paved path ends, look out for a very narrow path off to the left, down through the heather.

5 After about 100yds (90m) you will reach a concrete post where the path forks. Take the left fork and then follow the path down the gully to a fence beside a wall. Turn left here, forking left down another gully to reach a signpost by a wall and fence. Follow the sign left and then go over a spoil heap to reach a gate on your right.

6 Once through the gate, go straight down the hill through woodland. At the bottom cross a track to a stile by a gate and go down the lane. Just past some houses, where Whorl Hill Wood begins, take a footpath over two stiles and climb alongside the inside edge of the wood.

7 The track bends right with the perimeter of the wood and levels out. When you reach a T-junction, turn left and follow the track downhill to a stile and out of the woods. Go straight ahead through a gateway and follow a grassy track beside the farmhouse.

8 Go over a stile beside a gate and follow the track along the hillside. Go over a stile with steps beyond, turn left at the bottom and follow the field edge. Go over a waymarked stile by a gate and along the field. Walk along the field to reach a gate at the end and then follow the metalled lane passing Whorlton church and castle to return to Swainby village. To get to the Black Horse pub, turn right along the lane that traces the nearside bank of the stream.

Route facts

DISTANCE/TIME
6 miles (9.7km) 2h30

MAP OS Explorer OL26 North York Moors – Western

START Roadside parking in Swainby village, grid ref: NZ 477020

TRACKS Tracks and moorland paths, lots of bracken, 11 stiles

GETTING TO THE START
Swainby lies just off the busy A172 Teesside road 5 miles (8km) beyond the junction with the A19 and 12 miles (19.3km) due south of Middlesbrough. Turn south down the village street alongside the stream and park by the church. The Blacksmith's Arms lies on the corner at the north end of this street.

THE PUB The Black Horse, Swainby. Tel: 01642 700436; www.blackhorseswainby. co.uk

❶ Route finding could be difficult when the mists come down over the moors – it's best to save this route for settled weather.

HELMSLEY MAP REF SE6183

The handsome market town of Helmsley is where the National Park Authority has its administrative headquarters. Here too is a well-stocked Tourist Information Centre, in the castle, where visitors can browse for books, brochures and maps.

It may be only the size of a large village, but Helmsley has the purposeful, bustling, reassuring air of a county town. It is especially busy on Friday, which is market day. The old market cross on its stepped base is still in place, though the square is dominated by a more elaborate monument, designed by Sir Gilbert Scott to commemorate the second Lord Feversham.

A number of roads converge here; at one time this was an important halt on stagecoach routes. A regular service ran to London from the Black Swan Inn, which still has a large wooden swan in place of an inn sign.

These days more adventurous souls arrive with walking boots, cagoule and rucksack, for Helmsley is the starting point of the Cleveland Way, a 110-mile (176km) national trail that takes off across the moors before following the

coastal path down to Filey. Cleveland wayfarers should follow the 'acorn' signs up Castlegate, to get an excellent view of the castle standing 'head and shoulders' above the little town, before descending into Rye Dale and the atmospheric ruins of Rievaulx Abbey.

As is the case with many other North Yorkshire towns, behind Helmsley's prosperity is a castle and a prominent family. Of Walter l'Espec's first castle no traces now remain; the fortification we see today dates back to the 12th century. Robert de Roos was rewarded for his part in the Norman invasion by being given the manor of Helmsley. The de Roos family owned the castle until it was sold to Sir Charles Duncombe. Now it is in the care of English Heritage.

The castle was built for defence rather than show, yet it didn't witness any military action until the Civil War. It was here that the troops of Colonel Jordan Crossland, a loyal supporter of Charles I, were besieged by the Parliamentarian army of Sir Thomas Fairfax, which numbered a thousand troops. The siege, against what was regarded as one of the country's most impregnable fortresses, lasted three months. It might have lasted longer, but Royalist reinforcements were intercepted, and provisions confiscated. Crossland, forced to surrender, marched out of the castle on 22 November 1644, 'with colours flying and drums beating'.

While the Parliamentarian forces accepted this amicable surrender, they dismantled enough of the castle to ensure that it could never again be used by any side in a conflict. But they failed

■ **Insight**

DAYS GONE BY

Helmsley was a major stopping point on stagecoach routes in days gone by and it is easy to imagine weary passengers emerging gratefully from badly sprung coaches to avail themselves of victuals and refreshment at one of the many coaching inns that lined the Market Square. Some of these public houses are still giving hospitality to travellers – though today most of them arrive by car or motorcycle.

in their attempts to blow up the Norman castle keep, and the eastern wall still stands to its full height of 97 feet (30m), giving an idea of what an impressive fortification it had been.

The years have looked more kindly to Duncombe Park, just 1 mile (1.6km) southwest of Helmsley off the A170. Pride of place in these 600 tranquil acres (242ha) goes to the fine 200-room mansion designed by William Wakefield in 1713 as a fine family home for the Duncombe family and their descendants, the Fevershams. For 60 years the building was used as a girls' school, but in 1985 the present Lord and Lady Feversham took on the mammoth task of restoring the house and making it a family home once again. Now there is public access to both the house and the landscaped parkland, which boasts a delightful terrace walk, with Ionic and Tuscan temples to lend an air of romance. The temples and terrace were to have been linked by a coach drive, never completed, to the complementary Rievaulx Temple Terrace, also built by the Duncombe family.

KILBURN MAP REF SE5179

The village of Kilburn has two claims to fame, both of an artistic nature – the White Horse of Kilburn and woodcarver Robert Thompson.

The White Horse, a figure cut into the turf that gazes down from Roulston Scar, and a landmark for miles around, was created by teacher John Hodgson and his pupils in 1857. It is maintained by the Kilburn White Horse Association.

Visitors to Kilburn should not miss

■ **Insight**

A FASTIDIOUS VICAR
Charles Norris Gray was vicar of Helmsley from 1870 to the onset of World War I, and had a reputation as a doughty fighter for his chosen causes, which included the state of the drains, the dangers of wearing tight corsets and the lack of cleanliness among the lower orders. Who knows the state to which Helmsley might have degenerated without such a strong hand on the tiller? The vicarage was one of the many buildings whose restoration Gray supervised; today the building is the administrative centre of the National Park.

the workshops and showrooms of Robert Thompson, a woodcarver and cabinet-maker whose fame has travelled far and wide. Thompson was a self-taught craftsman whose skill remained largely unappreciated until he was commissioned to make some furniture for the local church. Encouraged by the results, Thompson began to specialise in ecclesiastical furniture. You will find that many Yorkshire churches have pews, pulpits and other fixtures made by him. One of the many pleasures of visiting them is to search for examples of the craftsman's trademark: a little carved mouse that stands proud from its surroundings. Many examples can be found in Kilburn's church, where a chapel was dedicated to the 'Mouseman' shortly before his death in 1958.

You can find Thompson's handiwork further afield – including York Minster and Westminster Abbey. Even without the mouse motif, you can recognise it by the heavy designs, the dark tones of the oak

■ Insight

THE 'MOUSEMAN'

Robert Thompson's signature, a carved mouse, can be found on all his pieces of furniture. But why a mouse? Thompson revealed in a letter that the idea came to him while working on a church screen. In conversation with another woodcarver he had mentioned that he was as poor as a church mouse. It seemed such an appropriate symbol that Thompson immediately adopted it for all his work.

■ Insight

THE INVITING MOORS

About 40 per cent of the National Park is heather moorland, comprising the largest expanse in England. To see the moors at their colourful best, a sea of purple, make your visit in the late summer months when the heather is in bloom. The hardy, black-faced Swaledale sheep are at home on the tops, and are brought down in to the valleys only at lambing times. Take care as you drive along the moorland ridge and roads, as the sheep have only the most rudimentary road sense and will dash into your path without warning.

wood and the rippled effect left by the adze (a heavy hand tool with an arched cutting blade set at a right-angle to the handle). This is furniture made to last not just a lifetime, but many lifetimes.

As the business quickly expanded, Thompson's own half-timbered house became a showroom. Behind the building are more recent workshops, in which a new generation of woodworkers follows in his footsteps. Those who can't afford one of the substantial pieces of furniture can find smaller wooden items

for sale, all featuring Thompson's famous mouse. You can see stacks of neatly piled oak planks outside the workshop, being seasoned before they are used. The outbuildings house an interesting small museum and exhibition centre.

A stream meanders through Kilburn, supplying part of its name: unusual, because here a stream is known as a beck rather than a burn. The 'burn' suffix is a clue that the origins of the village are Anglo-Saxon not Viking.

OSMOTHERLEY MAP REF SE4596

This handsome village, on the junction of roads old and new, is the starting point of a 42-mile (67km) route march across the moors to Ravenscar, known as the Lyke Wake Walk. Every weekend walkers decant from their cars, don boots and cagoules, and head for the high ground. The less energetic can stroll around the village; those who manage to work up an appetite will find excellent food on offer in the pubs that surround the old market place.

Northwest of Osmotherley is Mount Grace Priory (now in the care of the National Trust), though motorists need to make a rather inconvenient loop on the A19 dual carriageway to reach it. No matter – this is the best preserved of the nine Carthusian priories that were built in England. Typically, in most European monasteries the monks lived and worked together. The Carthusian Order was particularly strict, however; the monks not only shunned the outside world, they even avoided contact with each other.

Each monk (there were 24, including the prior) had a two-storey cell and walled garden to the back of it. Serving hatches adjacent to each cell door were ingeniously angled so that meals could be passed anonymously to the monks inside. The cells are grouped around the Great Cloister. While many of them rise no higher today than their foundations, one cell was reconstructed and furnished at the turn of the last century to show visitors how the monks would have lived their solitary lives.

The Carthusian Order was founded in 1048 by St Bruno of Reims, who took Christ's sojourn in the desert as the highest example for his monks to follow. They lived like hermits to avoid worldly distractions, with most of their day given over to prayer, study and contemplation. This harsh regime included a service in the middle of the night. Despite these privations, the Carthusian Order grew rapidly. As late as 1530 there was a waiting list for men who wished to join the Mount Grace community.

Mount Grace Priory was founded in 1398 by Thomas de Holland, with the agreement of Richard II. The monks were given land, which they rented out to tenant farmers. At the height of their wealth the income generated by the monks of Mount Grace was even greater than that of their Cistercian neighbours at Rievaulx Abbey. Yet the very success of the Carthusian communities contributed to their downfall. Henry VIII ordered them to be disbanded, and in 1539 the keys to Mount Grace Priory were handed to his representatives by John Wilson, the last prior.

Visitors now enter the priory through a manor house, built in 1654 on the site of an earlier gatehouse. It houses good exhibitions about the priory and the lives of its monks. The best preserved part of the priory is the old church, whose tower still stands to its original height. Compared with other monasteries, the church is small and simple.

■ Activity

A CHALLENGING WALK

The Lyke Wake Walk takes its inspiration from the old 'corpse roads', that crossed the moors, along which the deceased were carried to – often distant – burial grounds. Lyke refers to a corpse, as in a church lychgate; wake is the party after a funeral. This fine high-level walk, that lies between Osmotherley and Ravenscar, was begun in 1955 as a challenge walk – the challenge being to complete the 42 miles (67km) within 24 hours. However, the route has suffered erosion due to the pounding of too many walking boots.

■ Insight

THE HAMBLETON DROVE ROAD

The Hambleton Drove Road is a reminder of the days when drovers brought their cattle down from Scotland to sell at the English markets of York, Malton and beyond. This ancient ridgeway, as ruler-straight as a Roman road for much of its length, kept slow-moving cattle away from local herds and its wide verges offered free grazing. Just as importantly, the drovers were able to avoid the tolls charged for using the turnpike roads. Many sections of the Hambleton Drove Road have been incorporated into our modern road system. The Cleveland Way uses a section of the drove road, and is easily accessed from Osmotherley.

Byland Abbey and Olstead Observatory

Walk from the romantic ruins of Byland Abbey through lovely woodland to an old observatory at the highest point of the walk. The lumps and bumps of the final field you cross are the remains of the monks' ponds, some used for breeding fish.

Route Directions

1 From the car park, walk towards the Byland abbey ruins and then turn left along the lane at the abbey's north side. At a public footpath sign, go left and continue to walk up the drive of Abbey House and then right through a waymarked gate just before the house. After going through a second gateway bear slightly left, skirting a grassy bank towards the top left-hand corner of the field. Here you go though a waymarked gate and walk behind a bench seat. Now go through two more gates and on to a tarred lane just to the left of the buildings of Wass village.

2 Turn left. At a T-junction go through a gate signed 'Cam Farm, Observatory'. The path now climbs then leaves the wood edge to rise to a terrace. After a stile take the left-hand path, signed 'Cam Farm', to join a track climbing uphill to reach a forestry vehicle turning circle.

3 Turn right and, just before a waymarked metal gate at the edge of the forest, turn left along the inside wood edge (not waymarked). Follow the path, which soon bends left over wet ground to Oldstead Observatory. Pass to the left of the observatory and go down a slope to a track running steeply downhill. Take care here, as this path can be slippery!

4 Turn right along a track, signed 'Oldstead', then take a left turn at the next junction, over a stream where the path is joined by another track and becomes a tarred country lane. Then turn left at the T-junction to pass through the village of Olstead. Just before you reach the 'road narrows' sign, turn left.

5 Go through some gateposts and over a cattle grid. Then, as the avenue of trees ends, take a waymarked footpath to the right, and continue uphill

to a stile, before climbing a steep grassy bank. Note: this path can become overgrown with nettles, bramble and giant hogweed.

6 On reaching a tarred lane turn right, then take a track to the left by the Oldstead Grange sign. As you near the house, turn left towards some barns and wind your way through the farmyard to a stile by a metal gate. Bear half-right downhill on the track, then bend slightly right to a waymarked stile.

7 Ten yards/metres beyond the stile turn left and go through a wood to a Byland Abbey signpost. Follow the path as it leaves the woods and bends left beyond Cams Head Farm. Follow the hedge on the left, before going through a large gap. Now keep the hedge to the right.

8 The path crosses more fields with Byland Abbey directly ahead. In the last field veer left to follow the fence to a roadside stile. Turn left along the lane, then turn left again past The Abbey Inn to return to the car park.

Route facts

DISTANCE/TIME
5 miles (8km) 2h30

MAP OS Explorer OL26
North York Moors – Western

START Car park behind
Abbey Inn in Byland Abbey,
grid ref: SE 548789

TRACKS Woodland tracks,
field paths, 11 stiles

GETTING TO THE START
Byland Abbey is located
2 miles (3.2km) south of the
A170 road halfway between
Thirsk and Helmsley. It is
best reached by turning
south off the A170 3 miles
(4.8km) east of Sutton Bank.
In the village turn right by
the inn to access the signed
car park.

THE PUB The Abbey Inn,
Byland Abbey.
Tel: 01347 868678;
www.bylandabbeyinn.com

❶ In summer some paths
may be choked with nettles
and giant hogweed, so this
walk may be unsuitable for
small children.

Discover the Western Moors

A car tour from Helmsley through the western moors and dales, around the superb Cleveland and Hambleton Hills and taking in Rievaulx Abbey, Byland Abbey, Coxwold and Helmsley along the way. The best walking is around Chop Gate in Bilsdale, and Sutton Bank. A section of the tour is on narrow roads; please drive with care.

Route Directions

1 Begin the tour in Helmsley along the B1257, taking a left turning from the top of the square and a right turning by the church, signposted to 'Stokesley'. After 1.5 miles (2.4km), turn left down an unclassified road, signed 'Old Byland'. Immediately before a little bridge, turn right over the River Rye, to see the impressive ruins of Rievaulx Abbey ahead, in a delightful setting. Drive past the abbey, through Rievaulx village and sharply uphill to rejoin the B1257. Turn left, signed 'Stokesley'.

As you pass a conifer forest on your right, beautiful views open up of Bilsdale ahead. After the scattered houses of Chop Gate climb Hasty Bank with its viewpoint; look out on the right for the distinctive profile of Roseberry Topping.

2 At a mini-roundabout in Great Broughton turn left, signed 'Kirkby' and 'Carlton', with the escarpment of the Cleveland Hills rearing up on your left. Go through Kirby and Rusby, right at the T-junction, then left, on to the main A172 in the direction of Thirsk. After 2.5 miles (3.4km) turn left, signed 'Swainby'. Turn right over the bridge in the middle of Swainby, a pleasant village sitting astride a beck, and immediately left. Climb gradually uphill on to Scarth Wood Moor. Pass Cod Beck Reservoir and continue on into Osmotherley. Bear right, in the centre of the village, by the market cross, 'Northallerton and Thirsk'. Next to the stepped market cross is a curious stone table; market wares were probably displayed here. John Wesley certainly put it to good use as an open-air pulpit on the many occasions he preached in the town.

3 Turn right at the T-junction and on to the A19, signposted to 'Thirsk,' to join the dual carriageway southbound. Leave at the second turning on the left, signed 'Over Silton'. For the next few miles you are on very narrow roads, so please drive with care. Drive through Over Silton. At a T-junction a mile (1.6km) beyond, go left, signed 'Kepwick and Cowesby'. Drive uphill to a T-junction, which is adjacent to the gatehouse of Kepwick Hall; go right here, through the pleasant little village of Kepwick. Take the next turning on the left, signed 'Cowesby'. Drive through Cowesby (there is a sharp right bend in the village centre) to Kirby Knowle. Pass the parish church and turn left towards Felixkirk. Take the next two left turns, both signed 'Boltby'. Descend into Boltby, a happy arrangement of cottages in the honey-coloured stone so typical of this area.

4 Climb steeply out of the village and continue steeply again through Boltby Forest; at the top, turn right, signed 'Old Byland and Cold Kirby'. Follow this ruler-straight section of the route, part of the old Hambleton Drove Road – as you turn right you can see the old, unmetalled track continuing to the left. At the end of the road turn right

at a T-junction, signed to 'Thirsk and Sutton Bank'. Pass the car park at the top of Sutton Bank.
If you need to take a break and stretch your legs, this is the ideal spot – a waymarked path along the top of the bank offers easy walking and breathtaking views across the Vale of York and beyond.

5 Go left at a T-junction by the car park, on to the A170, signed 'Scarborough'. Take the first turning on the right, signed 'Yorkshire Flying Club, White Horse'. Drive downhill through woodland to the White Horse car park.
A short walk from here allows a closer investigation of the white horse, carved into the steep hillside in 1857 – though this is one landmark that looks better from a distance.

6 Continue on down to a T-junction; turn right to drive into the village of Kilburn. Look out for a half-timbered building: this is the furniture-making workshops and showroom founded by craftsman Robert Thompson.

6 Drive through the village; after 2 miles (3.2km) go left at a T-junction to arrive in the main street of Coxwold. Turn left at the crossroads at the bottom of the village, signed

'Byland Abbey Ampleforth and Helmsley'.
Laurence Sterne (author of *Tristram Shandy*) was once the vicar of Coxwold. Opposite to the church, Shandy Hall, his home which is now a museum devoted to his life and work.

8 Pass the evocative ruins of Byland Abbey, drive through Wass and on to Ampleforth

then pass Ampleforth Abbey with its famous Catholic public school. Oswaldkirk is next; once at the end of the village bear left, going steeply uphill, signed 'Helmsley'. At the top of the hill turn left, along the B1257 and right at the Trafalgar Arch at Sproxton, and you will soon return to Helmsley and the start of the tour.

OSWALDKIRK MAP REF SE6278

The village of Oswaldkirk is strung out along the road beneath the steep and well-wooded Oswaldkirk Bank, and looks out across the Ampleforth Valley. The community takes its name from St Oswald's parish church. St Oswald became King of Northumbria at the age of 30 in AD 634, and has a special place in the history of the Christian Church. What we know about St Oswald comes largely from the *Ecclesiastical History of the English People* written by the Venerable Bede in AD 731.

Oswald was deeply impressed by the monastic community on Iona, founded by St Columba. Once a Christian convert, he grafted the new faith on to familiar customs – for example, building Christian churches on sites of pagan worship. It was Oswald who gave the island of Lindisfarne to St Aidan and the monks of Iona as another sanctuary from which to spread Christianity.

One Easter, while Oswald and Aidan were about to share a meal, Oswald learned that there was not enough food to feed the poor at the gate. The king gave them his own food, still on its silver platter. Aidan was so moved by this act that he took the king's right hand and said 'May this hand never perish'.

Unfortunately, Oswald's faith could not save him from defeat in battle. He died in AD 642 while fighting the heathen King Penda of Mercia. Victorious Penda had Oswald's body dismembered and the pieces stuck on stakes. But, as prophesied, Oswald's right hand did not wither, and it was taken to Lindisfarne by Oswald's brother, Oswy, as a venerated relic. Thus began a cult, with Oswald being elevated to sainthood, and many tales of miraculous cures being associated with Oswald's bones.

The nave of St Oswald's church is largely Norman; cross fragments confirm that Oswaldkirk was already settled in Anglo-Saxon times. A couple of 'mother and child' sculptures in the porch offer an evocative contrast – one is modern, the other is Anglo-Saxon. Unusually, most of the rectors of Oswaldkirk are known by name; this practice started at the beginning of the 14th century and continues today.

RIEVAULX ABBEY
MAP REF SE5785

A short drive (or pleasant stroll) from Helmsley is one of Yorkshire's finest treasures. Today the setting of Rievaulx Abbey (English Heritage) is sheltered and inviting, but when Walter l' Espec dispatched a group of French monks to find a suitable site on which to build a new community it was reported to be fit only for 'wild beasts and robbers'. At that time there were no roads in the area; instead of neat copses and lush meadows there were only impenetrable thickets. To the devoutly ascetic Cistercian monks this part of the Rye Valley represented the sort of challenge on which they thrived.

In 1131, the monks began to build the mother church of the Cistercian Order in England. Many people today consider Rievaulx to be the pre-eminent Cistercian abbey in the country. The nave is Norman, while the rest of the abbey was built in the Early English style.

RIEVAULX ABBEY

◼ Insight

THE VILLAGE

The delightful little village of Rievaulx, with its thatched cottages of honey-coloured stone, grew up only after the Reformation. It is rather ironic that many of the houses were built from stone salvaged from the ruins of the abbey.

Enough remains of all the buildings to give visitors a very clear impression of what monastic life was like all those centuries ago.

The monks may have started out with a strictly ascetic attitude towards wealth and lifestyle; indeed the establishment of the Cistercian Order was partly due to what they considered to be the wicked corruption of the Benedictines orders. But the 140 monks and nearly 600 lay brothers of Rievaulx Abbey succeeded in creating a wealth and influence.

The monks farmed sheep, cultivated vegetables, ground corn and smelted iron, a process that required the felling of perhaps 40 trees to make a hundred-weight of metal. They even built canals to enable the iron to be transported. Stone for the buildings was brought to the site from local quarries by the same method. By 1538, when Henry VIII destroyed their way of life for ever with the Dissoution of Monasteries, the monks had become very wealthy indeed.

Cut into the hillside above the abbey is Rievaulx Terrace (National Trust), a curved grassy promenade that is more than a match for the landscaped terrace at nearby Duncombe Park. The terrace at Rievaulx was designed in 1758. It

offers strollers tantalising glimpses of the abbey between the groups of trees, with fantastic views of the Rye Valley and Hambleton Hills. There are temples, one in the Ionic style, with a fine sumptuous interior, the other Tuscan, to mark both ends of the terrace.

STOKESLEY MAP REF NZ5208

Now bypassed by the A172, Stokesley maintains the unhurried character of a market town. The broad verges of West Green create a little space between the Georgian façades of the houses and the main street that winds through the town. Stokesley still has regular markets, held every Friday on the cobbled edges of the main street. There are also busy livestock auctions and, each September, the market town is the site of one of the largest agricultural shows in the area.

The big open spaces include College Square and the market square. Behind them is Levenside, where the River Leven, little more than a stream at this point, follows its tranquil winding course between grassy banks and underneath a succession of little bridges. The oldest of these is the handsome arch of a fine old packhorse bridge; near by is a ford.

With the re-drawing of the county boundaries in 1974, Stokesley slipped into the county of Cleveland, though it has now been brought back into North Yorkshire. The National Park boundary makes a detour to exclude the town and neighbouring Great Ayton. While many of Stokesley's inhabitants commute to industrial Teesdale immediately to the north, Stokesley has, nevertheless, kept its own identity.

The Cleveland Hills form a backdrop to the south as you drive northeasterly direction along the A172 between Osmotherley and Stokesley. Once used by drovers, packhorse men, pedlars and monks visiting their outlying granges, the paths of the Cleveland Hills are now used by weekend walkers.

SUTTON BANK MAP REF SE5183

The view from the top of Sutton Bank is one of the finest in Yorkshire. Below you, spread out like a vast picnic blanket, is the flat plain of the Vale of York. It would be hard to imagine a sharper division between the rich, arable farmland that lies to the south and the heather moors of the Hambleton Hills immediately to the north. On a clear day, armed with a pair of binoculars, you can see York Minster and the Three Peaks of the Yorkshire Dales. Gormire Lake, directly below and almost hidden by trees, was once imagined to be bottomless.

The A170 marks its midway point between the market towns of Thirsk and Helmsley by making a long 1-in-4 climb to the top of Sutton Bank. You can watch cars and lorries labouring up what is one of the steepest stretches of road in the country. For those who want to stretch their legs and enjoy the view, or for those whose engines overheat, there is a car park (and information centre) conveniently sited at the top.

From here there is a splendid, and undemanding, walk along the edge of Sutton Bank. The Yorkshire Gliding Club operates from the top of the bank, and on summer weekends the sky will be filled with slim, silent planes exploiting the thermals rising up the scar. Powered planes tow the gliders over the edge – a moment that will moisten the palms of all but the most nonchalant of flyers. With the addition of microlight aircraft, hang-gliders and, of course, soaring birds, the skies beyond Sutton Bank can get very busy indeed.

The walk continues along the top of Roulston Scar, offering beautiful views all the way, to Kilburn's White Horse – a landmark which looks best from a distance. Thomas Taylor, a Kilburn man who made good in London, was so taken by the famous White Horse cut into the chalk downs near Uffington that he decided to create his own. He persuaded John Hodgson, a teacher from Kilburn School, to involve his pupils in the cutting of the figure. The main problem was that his chosen hillside, while suitably steep, was not chalk-based. Hodgson commandeered his pupils to help create the outline of a gigantic horse, and used gallons of whitewash to make the design stand out.

The White Horse of Kilburn is almost 325 feet (99m) from head to tail, and 227 feet (69m) high. Finished in 1857, it is now the only major landscape figure in the north of England. Whitewash fades in time, so these days chalk chippings are used. A White Horse Fund has been set up for the purpose of maintaining the horse, which is a very distinctive and much-loved landmark for miles around. There is another car park, directly beneath the White Horse, for those who don't want to walk too far. However you get to the horse, be careful not to damage the figure by walking on it.

The Hambleton Hills

Enjoy some of the north of England's best views and experience a bit of adventure with a ride along the edge of the escarpment. The long tarred lane that takes you north from Sutton Bank seems unremarkable, but there's a history dating back to the Iron Age tribes who settle here around 400 BC. They would have used the route long before the Romans followed in their footsteps.

Route Directions

1 Before you leave Sutton Bank Visitor Centre, take a look at the panoramas to the south and west. From here you can see for miles across the flat fields of the Vales of Mowbray and York. Alf Wight, alias the fictional vet James Herriot, believed this view to

be the finest in England. Apparently, both York Minster and Lincoln Cathedral are discernible on a clear day. From the visitor centre car park, turn left up the lane signed to Cold Kirby and Old Byland. Then take the left fork past Dialstone Farm and its

tall communications mast, before heading north on an ever-so-straight lane through cornfields and pastures.

2 The lane comes to a T-junction by a triangular wood, called the Snack Yate Plantation. This is a popular starting point for serious mountain bikers who will swoop down on rough tracks through Boltby Forest. Your route turns left down the lane. It's a gentle downhill for a short distance. Just before the road dives off the edge, turn left through a gate on to a grassy bridleway to cycle along the escarpment's edge. You are now riding on the Hambleton Hills. The first stretch is slightly uphill, but the track is firm and the views wide-sweeping. You'll see a small reservoir surrounded by forestry and the little village of Boltby huddled beneath a pastured hill.

3 The bridleway climbs to the top of the hill at High Barn, an old stone ruin shaded by a fine stand of sycamore. The going eases and the cliffs of an old quarry appear ahead. Here the bridleway goes through a gate on to a walled track for a short way. Ignore the bridleway on the left, which goes back to the Hambleton Road, and stay with the edge path to the hill above the rocks of Boltby Scar. This is the highest point of the ride. Note the wind-warped larch trees around here – they add to the views across the Vale of Mowbray.

4 The trees of the Boltby Forest now cover the west slopes, almost to the summit. Beyond the next offshoot bridleway, which you should ignore, the path becomes much narrower with a few embedded rocks in places. The difficulties are short-lived, but the younger and less experienced riders might prefer to dismount. The riding gets easier again as the bridleway arcs right above South Wood. At the end of this arc you turn left to a sign that tells you that the continuing edge path is for walkers only. This is a fine spot to linger and admire the views. To the south the half-moon-shaped Gormire Lake lies in a nest of broad-leaved woodland and beneath the sandy-coloured Whitestone Cliff.

5 When you've rested for a while, turn left on a bridleway to Dialstone Farm. This heads east across large prairie-like fields. Beyond a wood, the High Quarry Plantation, you will see the hurdles of the equestrian centre. Past the large farm, turn right along the tarred lane, then right again, back to the visitor centre car park.

Route facts

DISTANCE/TIME 7.4 miles (12km) 2h

MAP OS Explorer OL26 North York Moors – Western

START Sutton Bank Visitor Centre, grid ref: SE 516831

TRACKS Good level lanes followed by undulating bridleways on the edge of the escarpment

GETTING TO THE START Sutton Bank is situated 6 miles (9.7km) east of Thirsk. Take the A170 Scarborough turn-off from the A19 at Thirsk. This climbs the difficult road to Sutton Bank (caravans prohibited). The centre and car park are on the left at the top.

THE PUB The Hambleton Inn, Sutton Bank. Tel: 01845 597202; www.hambletoninn.co.uk

❶ A short section near Point 5 becomes narrower and with a few rocks in places. Inexperienced cyclists should dismount.

Out on the Tiles at Boltby and Thirlby Bank

The western boundary of the North York Moors National Park passes just outside Boltby. It is a delightful, small-scale place, with a tiny 19th-century chapel and stone-built houses, typical of the area. At the start of the walk you'll see a glittering mosaic of a kingfisher on a wall beside the Gurtof Beck. This is one of 23 that mark points on the Hambleton Hillside Mosaic Walk. Our route passes Tang Hall and Southwoods Hall before passing through Midge Holme Gate and into woodland. This is pheasant country, and you are likely to flush out one or two of these noisy birds during the walk. On the top of Boltby Scar, just as you begin the descent from the Cleveland Way you'll pass the scant remains of a Bronze Age hill fort.

Route Directions

1 From the humped-back bridge in the centre of Boltby, follow the signposted public footpath along the stream to a gate, and go through three more gates to pass over a small footbridge to a stile. Continue ahead, following the stream, going over another three stiles, to cross over a stone footbridge.

2 Continue to go across two stiles and then turn right to reach another stile beside a gateway. Continue ahead, crossing a plank across a drainage ditch. Cross the field to a stile and a stone bridge. At another stile in a crossing fence, go straight ahead through the next field to reach a waymarked gate. Continue along the side of the field to a wooden stile, then through a gate on to a metalled track.

3 Turn left and, at the end of the farm buildings, turn right by a sign to Southwoods and pass through a gate to go diagonally across the field. Bend left at a waymarked wooden gate to continue with a wire fence on your right. The path veers left and descends to another gate.

4 Continue through another gateway and past a house. Continue along the metalled track, and across a crossing track to a gate. Confusingly this old track is named Midge Holm Gate. Follow the track to reach another gate beside a cottage, Southwoods Lodge, and go on to a metalled lane.

5 Turn left here, following the track, then turn left up a public footpath, which is signposted to Thirlby Bank. This is a steep and often muddy track that ascends the ridge, past another public bridleway sign to reach a Cleveland Way sign at the top.

6 Turn left and then follow the long distance footpath for about a mile (1.6km) along the ridge, until you reach a public bridleway sign to the left, to Boltby. Descend to a gate then follow the woodland ride, crossing a track to a gate. Continue ahead down the field, go through a gate, and continue following the track round to the right.

7 At a signpost, turn right towards Boltby, to reach a gate. Pass a tree stump with a mosaic of a toadstool and go down to a gate on to a lane. Cross a footbridge and continue up the metalled lane. At the T-junction in the village, turn left to the hump-backed bridge.

Route facts

DISTANCE/TIME
5.25 miles (8.4km) 2h

MAP OS Explorer OL26 North York – Western

START Boltby village. Roadside parking in the village, grid ref: SE 490866

TRACKS Mostly easy field and woodland paths; one steep, muddy climb; 10 stiles

GETTING TO THE START
At Thirsk head to the A19 heading south and then turn left onto the A170 Pickering and Scarborough road. After around 2.5 miles (4km) take the left turn signposted to Thirlby and Boltby. Boltby is about 3 miles (5km) after the turn off.

THE PUB The Carpenter's Arms, Felixkirk (located southwest of Boltby). Tel: 01845 537369; www.carpentersarmsfelixkirk.co.uk

❶ Very steep and muddy climb up Thirlby Bank.

■ TOURIST INFORMATION CENTRES

Helmsley
Helmsley Castle.
Tel: 01439 770173
Sutton Bank
Tel: 01845 597426

■ PLACES OF INTEREST

There will be an admission charge at the places of interest unless otherwise stated.

Byland Abbey
Coxwold.
Tel: 01347 868614
Duncombe Park
Helmsley. Tel: 01439 770213;
www.duncombepark.com
Helmsley Castle
Tel: 01439 770442
Helmsley Walled Garden
Tel: 01439 771427; www.
helmsleywalledgarden.org.uk
Mount Grace Priory
Osmotherley.
Tel: 01609 883494
Newburgh Priory
Tel: 01347 868372;
www.newburghpriory.co.uk
Rievaulx Abbey
Rievaulx.
Tel: 01439 798228
Rievaulx Terrace
Rievaulx.
Tel: 01439 798340
Shandy Hall
Coxwold.
Tel: 01347 868465

■ SHOPPING

MARKETS
Helmsley and Stokesley
Open-air market, Fri.
LOCAL SPECIALITIES
Furniture and Gifts
The Mouseman Visitor
Centre, Kilburn.
Tel: 01347 869100;
www.robertthompsons.co.uk

■ OUTDOOR ACTIVITIES

BIKE HIRE
Oswaldkirk
Golden Square Campsite,
Oswaldkirk.
Tel: 01439 788269
LONG-DISTANCE FOOTPATHS
The Cleveland Way
A 110-mile (176km) walk
from Helmsley to Filey Brigg.
The Lyke Wake Walk
A 42-mile (67km) walk from
Osmotherley to Ravenscar.
HORSE-RIDING
Boltby
Boltby Trekking Centre,
Johnstone Arms.
Tel: 01845 537392;
www.boltbytrekking.co.uk
Hawnby
Bilsdale Riding Centre,
Shaken Bridge Farm.
Tel: 01439 798252;
www.horseholiday.co.uk

■ ANNUAL EVENTS & CUSTOMS

Bilsdale
Bilsdale Show, Chop Gate,
Aug.
Coxwold
Coxwold Fair, Jun
Helmsley
Ryedale Festival, Jul/Aug.
Kilburn
Kilburn Feast, early to
mid-Jul.
Osmotherley
Summer Games, early Jul.
Osmotherley Show, Aug.
Stokesley
Stokesley Show, Sep.

Tea Rooms

Lord Stone's Café
Carlton Bank Car Park,
Chop Gate, TS9 7LQ.
Tel: 01642 778227
This one of Britain's very few
underground cafés. Inside
you'll find that the rock-hewn
room behind the conventional
café façade there's a warm
welcome and some good food,
from delicious home-made
soups and corned-beef pie to
cakes and pastries. You can
also get draft beer, too – or
try the spring water; it's cool,
clear and free!

Coxwold Tearooms
School House, Coxwold,
YO61 4AD.
Tel: 01347 868077; www.
coxwoldschoolhouse.co.uk
You can eat in either of the
two rooms, one very cosy and
the other airy, or outside in
the tea garden. You can treat
yourself to afternoon tea with
home-baking, or sample the
delights of Yorkshire ham-
and-eggs.

The Castlegate Bakery and Café
12 Castlegate, Helmsley,
YO6 5AB.
Tel: 01439 770304
Two of the specialities here
are Yorkshire Curd Tarts and
traditional Yorkshire Parkin,
both made in the bakery

alongside. The traditional
café serves a generous
cream tea with its home-
made scones, or try the
celebrated steak pie.

The Angel Café Tearoom
22 High Street, Stokesley
TS9 5QD. Tel: 01642 713622
A traditional town-centre tea
room set on the handsome
main street. There's a small
area with sofas at the front of
the premises, with tables
behind. All the cakes and
scones are home-made;
locals make a bee-line for
the coffee cake. The Angel
also serves a range of full
meals and snacks.

Pubs

The Black Swan Inn
Oldstead, Coxwold,
YO61 4BL. Tel: 01347 868387;
www.theblackswaninn.com
This is a proper country pub
with a relaxed and welcoming
atmosphere. As you'd expect
there is real ale available in
the Drovers Bar, with its
flagged floor, comfy chairs
and a bar made by Robert
Thompson's craftsmen in
nearby Kilburn. There's a
pretty garden, and views of
woodland and hills. The food
is freshly prepared from local
ingredients and includes a
particularly impressive
choice for vegetarian diners.

The Golden Lion
6 West End, Osmotherley,
DL6 3AA. Tel: 01609 883526
Furnished with wooden
flooring and benches, this
charming pub offers a wide
range of ales, both local and
imported. There is a superb
menu, from excellent pub
food through to top-notch
cuisine. The home-made
burgers are delicious, and
there's a good selection of
fish, as well as a tasty steak
and kidney pie.

The Hare Inn
Scawton, YO7 2HG.
Tel: 01845 597524
This is a great place to relax,
with a drink in the charming
low-beamed bar (real ales,
including guest beers) or a
meal in the adjoining dining
area. Make sure you leave
room for a pudding – you'll
find the lemon possett,
among others, is excellent.

The Wombwell Arms
Wass, YO61 4BE.
Tel: 01347 868280
There are two bistro-style
restaurants, serving a menu
that includes steak and
Guinness pie, as well as
plenty of local produce and
fish. The bars stock a good
range of Yorkshire ales,
including Black Sheep and
Timothy Taylor's.

Central Moors

The central moors include high moorland, beautiful valleys and some delectable villages. The North Yorkshire Moors Railway runs through the wooded Newtondale Gorge on the edge of Cropton Forest, which offers a host of leisure possibilities, from energetic cycling and riding through to easy strolls and quiet picnics. To the north of the forest is Roman Road on Wheeldale, a well-preserved section of road thought to be of Roman origin.

Westerdale

326
Pike Hill

369

Church
Houses
Thorgill
6
Wheeldale ☆
Rosedale Abbey
Low Mill
290
Stape
*Cropton
Forest* ☆

*North Riding
Forest Park*

Hutton-
le-Hole
5
Lastingham
Gillamoor
Newton-on-
Rawcliffe
Spaunton
Fadmoor
Cropton
Cawthorn
Appleton-
le-Moors

Kirkbymoorside

Wrelton
Aislaby
A170
Sinnington
Middleton

Wombleton

Marton

Normanby

Salton
Nunnington
Great
Barugh
East
Ness
Brawby
Stonegrave
Butterwick
Hovingham
B1257
Slingsby

5 Walk start point

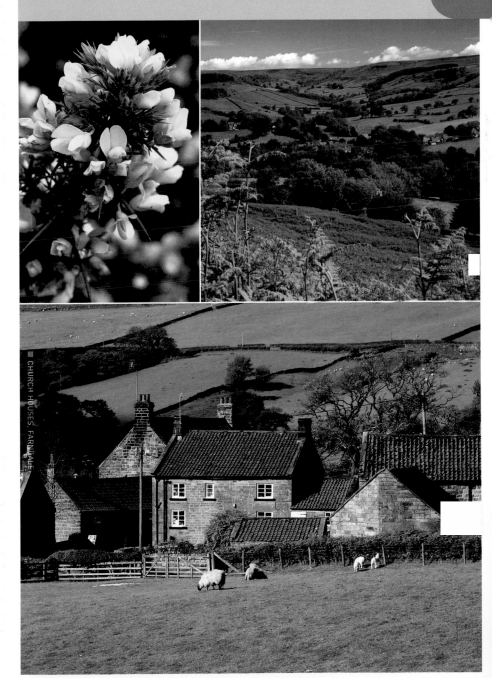

CHURCH HOUSES, FARNDALE

Unmissable attractions

Discover the remains of the Roman road on Wheeldale Moor...visit Nunnington Hall to see the miniature rooms...walk across the moors to Lilla Cross, the oldest on the Moors...climb the one-in-two hill called Rosedale Chimney out of Rosedale Abbey... sit quietly in the crypt at Lastingham church for an experience of early history...hire a bike and follow the track of the former Rosedale Railway...have lunch at the Spa Tea rooms of Hovingham Bakery...visit Farndale in spring for the superb display of wild daffodils...take the road across the moors from Rosedale Abbey to Egton Bridge when the heather is blooming...have dinner in the garden at the famed Star Inn at Harome...travel through Newtondale Gorge on the North Yorkshire Moors Railway.

1 Nunnington Hall
The lovely old manor house of Nunnington Hall dates mainly from the 17th century. It is set in beautiful gardens on the banks of the River Rye.

2 Chimney Bank
Wonderful scenery unfolds from the top of snow-capped Chimney Bank, between the villages of Rosedale Abbey and Hutton-le-Hole.

3 Cyclists at snow-covered Rosedale
Cycling the quiet back roads over the central moors is a popular way to explore the National Park, whatever the season.

4 Ryedale Folk Museum
An amazing collection of rural buildings rescued from all around the North York Moors have been reconstructed in a hamlet setting behind the modest entrance to this museum of local life.

5 Rosedale Abbey Sundial
As the name of the village suggests, Rosedale Abbey was once the site of a small Cistercian priory founded in 1158. Little remains of the original building (the stone was reclaimed for building houses in the village and the new church) except a turret staircase and a sundial.

CROPTON FOREST

The moors are continually evolving, and one of the most dramatic changes of the 20th century was the creation of large-scale conifer plantations. The Forestry Commission began the process in the 1920s; now the area comprises one of the most extensive man-made forests n the country. Cropton Forest occupies a large area of the North Riding Forest Park between Rosedale in the west and Newtondale to the east.

■ Activity

BACK TO NATURE

The recreational possibilities of Cropton Forest are now being realised. On any summer weekend you will see mountain bikers tackling the forest trails, walkers following well-waymarked footpaths and families enjoying themselves at the many picnic sites and adventure playgrounds. Those who prefer their nature 'red in tooth and claw' will head for the solitude of the breezy moor-tops. The Newtondale Horse Trail, offers 35 miles (56km) of bracing, traffic-free riding. Local riding stables hire out horses by the hour or day.

■ Insight

MAULEY CROSS

Moorland crosses are generally reliable indicators that an old thoroughfare, or crossroads, is near at hand. Mauley Cross stands on the route of one of the oldest known roads across the moors to have survived, which may date from Roman times. The cross stands where the track meets the medieval Brown Howe Road. It is named after the de Mauley family of Mulgrave Castle near Whitby and probably marked the limits of grazing rights. The cross once stood on open moorland.

Conifer planting on this scale has not met with universal approval; many feel that well-loved views have been unfairly smothered beneath the starkly dark geometric shapes of these plantations. Nevertheless, the afforestation of what had mostly been moorland and poor-quality farmland brought much-needed employment to many rural areas.

The woodlands are now reaching maturity, and upwards of 120,000 tonnes of timber are felled every year to meet consumer demand for softwoods. More recently, greater care has been taken to ensure that plantings harmonise with their surroundings. Areas of broadleaved and mixed woods provide a more varied habitat for wildlife, and are easier on the eye than vast conifer plantations.

Cropton Forest provides plenty of outdoor activities – there is a campsite, forest cabins and educational outdoor activity centres set out amid the trees, and plenty of opportunities for walking and biking. The North Yorkshire Moors Railway, from Pickering to Grosmont, passes through the eastern edge of the forest, and stations at Levisham and Newtondale provide easy access for visitors to the woodland.

Roman roads are not hard to find, on the map at least. The Roman road, commonly known as Wade's Causeway, across Wheeldale Moor, is immediately to the north of Cropton Forest, is still that rare thing – a Roman road which is still visible on the ground.

There are Roman remains to be seen at Cawthorn Camp, which is believed to have been as a training camp, which is signposted from the minor road between the villages of Cropton and Newton-on-Rawcliffe. From the purpose-built car park the waymarked path, no more than a mile (1.6km) long, guides you around them. The well-preserved earthworks reveal a camp, two forts and an annexe wedged side by side on a plateau, which enjoys panoramic views to the north across Cropton Forest to the moors beyond. By the year AD 122, when the Emperor Hadrian was constructing his famous wall to the north, the Cawthorn camps had been abandoned.

FARNDALE

Farndale is a delightful valley at any time of the year, but every Eastertime it blooms with a profusion of golden wild daffodils. The daffodil walk accompanies the River Dove between Low Mill and Church Houses. This is an undeniably pleasant stroll, and suitable for wheelchairs, but try to pick a weekday, if possible, to make your visit; or venture a little further afield, for wild daffodils can be found throughout the valley. The traffic has become so heavy in recent years that a field in the village of Low Mill becomes a car park while the daffodils are in bloom. There is a park-and-ride bus service operating from Kirkbymoorside and Hutton-le-Hole.

But why Farndale? And why in such profusion? Farndale's blooms are wild, short-stemmed daffodils; stories variously attribute their planting to the monks of Rievaulx, and to Father Postgate, a Catholic priest who was persecuted for his faith. We merely know that wild daffodils have flourished in these dales for centuries.

■ Insight

SARKLESS KITTY

The dales are rich in folklore; one story tells of Kitty Garthwaite, 'Sarkless Kitty', from the village of Lowna Bridge, who, more than 200 years ago, was 'walking out' with Willie Dixon of Hutton-le-Hole. A rumour came to Kitty that Willie was seeing another lass. A lovers' tiff by the River Dove was followed, tragically, by Kitty's being found drowned in a pool, wearing only her 'sark', or petticoat. After their argument, Willie had ridden to York to get a marriage licence. On his return his horse stumbled and Willie drowned in the same pool where Kitty had earlier been found. The ghost of Kitty, naked but carrying her sark over her arm, began to haunt the riverside spot where the lovers had kept their trysts.

The greatest threat to the daffodils has been the ever-increasing numbers of visitors, who were once unable to admire the spectacular springtime displays without gathering armfuls of the flowers. Once market traders found this free source of daffodils the flowers were in danger, and in 1953 about 2,000 acres (810ha) of Farndale were designated as a nature reserve; the daffodils are safe for us all to enjoy. Resist the temptation to pick any.

At other times of the year Farndale reverts to being a peaceful farming community. Both sides of the valley are accessible; from either Kirkbymoorside and Hutton-le-Hole on the A170 to the south, or, most dramatically, from the north down a steep road which descends from Blakey Ridge just to the south of the Lion Inn.

HOVINGHAM MAP REF SE6675

One of North Yorkshire's prettiest villages, Hovingham, lies on the route of an old Roman road from Malton to Boroughbridge. When the foundations of Hovingham Hall were being laid, in 1745, Roman remains were unearthed, including part of a bath house. The Hall's first owner, Sir Thomas Worseley, was a descendant of Oliver Cromwell. His passion for horses led him to build the stable block facing on to the village green. In a rather unusual arrangement, visitors have to pass through the stable block to reach the Hall's main entrance. The Hall is mainly open to private parties by arrangement.

The attractive architectural unity of the surrounding houses, the neat layout with broad grass verges and an air of gentility all mark Hovingham out as an estate village. One of the Hall's lawns is today the village's cricket pitch; surely one of the loveliest grounds on which to watch or play the summer game. The houses at the northern end of the village are clustered either side of a pretty little beck, with a ford, where ducks swim and await visitors who may have stale bread to feed to them.

HUTTON-LE-HOLE
MAP REF SE7090

It is to Hutton-le-Hole's benefit that it lies just off the main A170 between Thirsk and Scarborough, for it, unlike its larger neighbours, has managed to maintain its distinct personality instead of selling its soul to the tourist trade. One of Yorkshire's 'picture postcard' villages, its houses are set back from

Hutton Beck, a little watercourse spanned by a succession of pretty little bridges. The village green is the size of a meadow, but the grass is cropped short by grazing sheep, which wander wherever they choose – as likely as not in the middle of the road.

The houses of discreet grey stone, with the red-tiled roofs so typical of the moors, lend a timeless air to the village. The tiny church has some very fine oak furniture made by Robert Thompson the of Kilburn; a close examination will reveal the trademark carved mouse that can be found on his work.

Once you have seen the village, don't neglect to visit Ryedale Folk Museum. This open-air collection is based on the displays of bygones built up by two local collectors. From its beginnings in a single old farm building, the museum has expanded far beyond its walls, to include many other vernacular buildings – brought stone by stone to the museum and painstakingly re-erected.

For nearly 500 years a thatched, cruck-framed cottage has stood here in Danby village. In 1967 this typical farmer's house was moved to the museum's 2.5-acre (1ha) site. The tall, 16th-century manor house, also thatched and cruck-framed, is a huge hall open to the roof beams. This was once the meeting place of the Manor Court, where disputes were settled and common rights safeguarded. Other museum buildings house a primitive 16th-century glass furnace, a photographer's studio, and a row of shops recreated as they would have looked more than a hundred years ago.

■ Insight

RYEDALE'S WITCH POST

The cruck-framed house at the Ryedale Folk Museum contains one of the rare examples of a witch post to have survived – most of which are found in the north of England. This post, of mountain ash, is elaborately carved with a cross and other, more ambiguous, symbols. It stands by the fireplace, so it would be passed by anyone who came into the living area, and also had the practical purpose of supporting the beam across the inglenook. It was designed, of course, to ward off evil spirits and protect those who sat here enjoying the fire's warmth.

■ Insight

ST GREGORY'S SUNDIAL

The engraved inscription on the sundial at St Gregory's Minster is in Old English. Translated it reads 'Orm, the son of Gamal, bought St Gregory's Church when it was utterly broken down and fallen, and he rebuilt it from ground level, to Christ and St Gregory, in the days of King Edward and Earl Tostig. Howarth made me and Brand the priest. This is sun's marker at all times'. The Edward of the inscription is King Edward the Confessor, who ruled between 1042 and 1066; Tostig became Earl of Northumberland in 1055; Howarth made the sundial; Brand was the name of the parish priest. This brief inscription is the longest example of Anglo-Saxon carving to have survived.

■ Insight

CRUCK-FRAMED HOUSES

The crucks and their cross-beams made a shape like the letter 'A'; these heavy timbers supported the entire weight of the building's roof, allowing the walls to be infilled. Since the walls were not load bearing, it was an easy matter to alter the position of doors, or create extra windows.

Throughout these buildings, exhibits in their own right, are informal displays showing what life was like in such moorland villages in bygone days. The site is also the venue for various events which are held through the year.

KIRKBYMOORSIDE

MAP REF SE6986

The market town of Kirkbymoorside lies on the edge of the moors just outside the National Park, on the A170 between Helmsley and Pickering. Don't judge the place by first appearances; you should leave the main road to investigate the old heart of the town. The broad main street is lined with inns, a reminder that Kirkbymoorside was an important halt in the days of stage coaches. The oldest inn is the Black Swan, whose elaborately carved entrance porch bears the date 1632. The market cross, mounted on a stepped base, can be found in a side street near by. Market day is Wednesday, as it has been since medieval times.

Kirkbymoorside has a road called Castlegate. Once it had a castle too, on a hill behind the parish church, but stones salvaged from its ruins were used to build the 17th-century tollbooth in the market place. Another fortified building was once a hunting lodge built by the Neville family. The church, though old, was largely rebuilt last century.

Lovers of beautiful old churches should rejoin the A170 and travel westwards in the direction of Helmsley for just a few hundred yards, before following the sign for St Gregory's Minster. If the word 'minster' conjures up some grand edifice, you will be surprised to find a tiny, dignified church built of grey stone, almost hidden away in beautiful, secluded Kirkdale.

This ancient building was dedicated to St Gregory – the pope who dispatched St Augustine to preach Christianity to the pagan English in AD 597. There has long been a church here, certainly before Anglo-Saxon times, as it had to be rebuilt in c1060, perhaps as a result of Viking destruction. Recent excavations have revealed a prehistoric standing stone by the west tower, evidence of Christians reusing a pagan site. Many visitors ask: why a minster? And why here, in such an isolated spot? The term 'minster' is derived from the Latin monasterium, which denoted a community of priests or monks who used the church as a base from which to serve the surrounding countryside before the parish system evolved. This status has remained with churches; some like this one are small, some like York Minster are large and important.

We can be more certain about the dates of the rebuilding because ancient – yet tantalisingly brief – details are carved on a sundial mounted over the south door. The sun doesn't reach it any more; to protect the sundial, the best Anglo-Saxon example known, a porch was added in the 19th century.

LASTINGHAM MAP REF SE7290

The casual visitor to the small village of Lastingham will see a collection of good-looking houses, a few wellheads and a welcoming inn, but Lastingham has something more to offer – a unique place in the history of Christianity.

St Cedd left the island of Lindisfarne (Holy Island) in AD 655 and chose this site on which to build a monastery. It was an area which, according to the Venerable Bede, was 'the lurking place of robbers and wild beasts'. St Cedd was buried in his monastery, close to the altar. This early building was later sacked by invading Danes.

In 1078 Abbot Stephen of Whitby moved his own community to Lastingham. He built a crypt dedicated to St Cedd, in which the saint's remains were re-interred. Apart from cosmetic changes (and the stairs leading down into it from the nave of the church above) the crypt looks the way it did almost a thousand years ago.

Itself a church in miniature, the crypt has a chancel, aisles, an eastern apse, stout Norman pillars, a low vaulted roof and a stone slab for an altar. Here, too, are fragments of ancient crosses. It was to have been part of a large abbey, but Abbot Stephen's plans were thwarted and the community moved to the larger site of St Mary's Abbey, York.

The present church, planned merely as the abbey's chancel, was eventually consolidated to meet local needs; the congregation was derived from those who lived in many of the surrounding villages. Today, visitors to Lastingham's church come from further afield to see a building that has happily survived years of neglect and clumsy 'restorations'. A closer examination of two of the village's wellheads reveal that one is dedicated to St Cedd, the other to his more famous brother, St Chad, who succeeded him as Abbot of Lastingham.

Lastingham and Hutton-le-Hole

From Lastingham and St Cedd's monastery the walk reaches Spaunton before leading on to Hutton-le-Hole clustered around an irregular green and along the banks of a beck. The route passes through fields and woodland on the return leg.

Route Directions

1 From The Blacksmiths Arms walk back down to the village green and turn left, following signposts to Cropton, Pickering and Rosedale. Where the road swings left, go right along a lane to wind over a small bridge and beside a stream. Ascend to a footpath sign, and go right, uphill, through a gate and through woodland to a handgate on to a road. Take the upper right fork lane, signed 'Spaunton'.

2 Follow the road through Spaunton, and bend right at the end of the village, then turn left by the public footpath sign over the cattle grid into the farmyard. The waymarked track curves through the farm to reach another footpath sign, where the track bends left. At a large outbuilding the track bends left again.

3 After about 200yds (185m), follow a public footpath sign right and walk on to another sign as the track bends left. After 100yds (91m) take a footpath to the right, down the hill into woodland. Where the path divides, take the left fork down to a stile on your right, going off the track and down a steep grassy path into the valley. Descend beside a stream to a stile by a gate, which takes you on to the road in Hutton-le-Hole.

4 Turn right up the main street. After passing the Barn Hotel and the Wychwood Gifts shop turn right, following a route signed to Lastingham. Beyond a gate, pass through a garden and to the right of some sheds to reach a stile, which gives entry to a large field which is sometimes used

as a campsite. Turn left and follow the edge of the field and over two more stiles to a kissing gate before a footbridge. Follow the path now through woodland to a gate and take the grassy track to the road.

5 Turn right and follow the road for 0.5 mile (800m) and turn left at a footpath sign just before the road descends to a stone bridge. A rutted track bends right running between farmland on the right and Spaunton Moor.

6 Just before Camomile Farm, leave the track on the left and follow the footpath sign and waymarker posts to round a copse of sycamores, beyond which you descend into a valley. Cross over the stream to a stile and a kissing gate. Continue walking with the wall on your right-hand side to another kissing gate and stile, which will lead you to a carved stone with a cross and a three-pointed sign.

7 Turn right, downhill, through a gate and on to the metalled road that descends to the village of Lastingham.

Route facts

DISTANCE/TIME
4.5 miles (7.2km) 2h

MAP OS Explorer OL26 North York Moors – Western

START Village street in Lastingham, grid ref: SE 729905

TRACKS Farm tracks and field paths, 8 stiles

GETTING TO THE START
Lastingham is reached by turning north from the A170 Thirsk to Scarborough road between Kirkby Mills and Sinnington. Park on the village street. Turn left by the church to visit The Blacksmith Arms.

THE PUB The Blacksmiths Arms, Lastingham. Tel: 01751 417247

❶ Route finding could be difficult when the mists come down over the moors – save this route for settled weather.

NUNNINGTON MAP REF SE6679

At Nunnington a delightful 17th-century three-arched bridge spans the River Rye. From one of its embrasures (the V-shaped spaces constructed to shield pedestrians from the traffic) you can gaze down into the water and try to spot basking trout, superbly camouflaged against the sandy river bed. Set in beautiful gardens across the river is honey-coloured Nunnington Hall. This tranquil setting offers no clue to the hall's turbulent past; this isn't one of those stately homes that cruised serenely through the centuries, while leaving barely a ripple.

Nunnington Hall's early history is sketchy; it is thought to have been built on the site of a nunnery – hence its name. It passed through many hands, including the Abbot of St Mary's, York. Another later owner, Viscount Preston, served James II as Secretary of State for Scotland; charged later with treason, he escaped the gallows only by implicating his fellow conspirators.

While the hall's west wing can be dated to 1580, most of the building, a concoction of Tudor and Stuart styles, was built during the 17th century. The Hall, housing the entrancing Carlisle collection of miniature rooms and a display by the British Toymakers Guild, is now cared for by the National Trust.

Nunnington's handsome houses in grey stone are hidden from sight to those who drive straight through the village; it's better to explore on foot. Nunnington's church, with its double dedication to St James and All Saints, dates largely from the 13th century.

Here, in an alcove, is the effigy of a knight in chain mail. This recumbent figure commemorates Sir Walter de Teyes, Lord of the Manor of Nunnington and Stonegrave until his death in 1325.

ROSEDALE

Rosedale is a lovely tranquil valley today, echoing with the bubbling cry of the curlew and the distant barking of farm dogs. City visitors will feel themselves to be a long way from the noise and grime of Yorkshire's industrial heartlands. But appearances can be deceptive. Just one hundred years ago the scene was very different: Rosedale was a veritable moorland 'Klondike'.

Ironstone had been mined here, sporadically, since the Iron Age. During the 13th century mining added to the wealth of the monks of Byland Abbey; but it was only in the middle of the 19th century that the extent of Rosedale's subterranean wealth was realised, with the discovery of massive quantities of top-grade iron ore. The Industrial Revolution brought a huge demand for iron; the blast furnaces on the Rivers Tees and Tyne needed a constant supply for building ships, railways and general engineering. Other mines were driven – at Glaisdale, Beck Hole and on the coast, for example – but the mines at Rosedale proved to be the most productive.

The transport of ore was difficult from isolated Rosedale. In 1861 the North Eastern Railway Company built a line from Battersby Junction on the Stockton–Whitby line, over the bleak moorland to Rosedale West. In 1865 a branch was built around the head of

Rosedale to the east mines, joining the original line at Blakey Junction, just below the Lion Inn on Blakey Ridge. To reach Teesside the wagons, now laden with ore, were winched down the steep descent of the Ingleby Incline. The engines that plied the high-level line between the Rosedale mines and the incline never came down from their moorland heights, except when they had to be repaired.

The Rosedale railway was closed in 1929, by which time the valley's mining boom was over. Though the demand for iron was as buoyant as ever, ore could be mined more cheaply elsewhere. The route of this fascinating line is used today by walkers, cyclists and horse riders. The valley is quietly 'going back to nature', but the massive calcining kilns (where ironstone was roasted to reduce its weight) are being preserved, so that Rosedale's mining past will not be forgotten.

You will search in vain for the abbey that gave the village of Rosedale Abbey its name. The ladies who serve in the tea shops answer the question with a weary resignation that suggests this is not the first time they've been asked. The truth is that you can see the remains of the abbey (it was actually a priory) wherever you look: the population explosion of the mid-19th century meant that the priory was plundered for its building stone to build homes for the ironstone miners. Whether this is seen as the desecration of a religious site, or the sensible recycling of a valuable resource, depends on your own reading of history. The priory was founded in 1158 as a Cistercian nunnery by William of Rosedale. It was never a large establishment: there were probably only nine nuns and a prioress living here.

St Lawrence's Church stands on the site of the priory's chapel. To find a couple of relics from the earlier building, walk up to the altar rail. One of the stones set into the floor here bears a carved cross and, faintly, the name Maria, in memory of one of the nuns. Beyond the altar rail is an ancient stone seat from the nunnery; it is carved from a single block of stone.

■ Insight

YORKSHIRE'S 'KLONDIKE'
Between 1850 and 1870 the population of Rosedale quadrupled, as the mines were driven deep into the valley sides. A system of underground passages was dug, consolidated by wooden supports. The miners excavated to either side of these tunnels, with pick and shovel, to win the ore-bearing rock. The news soon spread, with experienced miners converging on Rosedale from all over the country – and particularly from Cornwall and Wales. At the height of production, more than 5,000 men found work here.

■ Activity

CYCLING IN ROSEDALE
The old Rosedale railway is ideal for cycling for much of its length, as it is relatively level and surfaced with ash ballast. The best section is from Rosedale Bank Top to Blakey Junction, near the Lion Inn (4 miles/6.8km) and then across the moors to Ingleby Bank Top, another 7 miles (11.9km). You could even cycle down the incline – but remember what goes down must come up again.

STANDING STONES

It is appropriate that Ralph Cross should have been chosen as the emblem of the National Park, for standing stones and wayside crosses are one of the most intriguing features of the moors. No other area of the country can boast so many examples.

Within the National Park boundary there are more than a thousand stones raised by man, standing witness to many centuries of settlement on the moors. The moorland stones are known as 'crosses', even though only a small proportion of them are actually carved into the shape of a cross. Some are simple monoliths fitted with side-pieces to make a cruciform shape. One particular design, repeated in many moorland crosses, is known as the wheelhead. It consisted of a widening of the top of a stone, which is pierced with four holes to create the shape of a cross. Other stones simply have the design of a cross carved into their surface.

The moorland crosses weren't erected at random; they were put up for a variety of reasons. A number of them were preaching crosses, marking the spot where itinerant monks would attempt to bring the gospel to the pagan Anglo-Saxon communities. If the monks were successful and their words fell on willing ears, a church might be built on, or near, the site of the preaching cross.

In the Middle Ages other crosses were put up as waymarkers, to guide travellers across the largely featureless expanses of 'Blackamore'. Moorland roads were established by usage; they weren't 'built' like the Roman roads; at

best, the routes might be delineated by a line of causeway stones. The moorland crosses would help to mark the route, and offer weary travellers further targets in the distance to aim for. Other crosses were erected to mark the boundaries of the monastic sheep-grazing land.

During these times the building of bridges and wayside crosses was seen as an act of piety. Many rich men would attempt to improve their chances of getting into heaven by providing money for such good works. So, here too, a stone shaped as a cross would reflect both the donor's good intentions and the travellers' gratitude to find another waymark. It's hard for us, in our cars, to

■ Visit

EARLY SIGNPOSTS

Stone signposts were erected at all the crossroads on the moors in 1711 by order of the Justices at Northallerton, to prevent travellers from getting hopelessly lost. They sign the direction of each road to the nearest main town, and sometimes the distances. The spelling is distinctly idiosyncratic, and some have primitive hands carved on them. There is a good example about 2 miles (3.2km) north out of Hutton-le-Hole on the road to Ralph Cross at map reference SE 693926.

■ Activity

THE CROSSES WALK

The Crosses Walk is a challenge walk of about 53 miles (84.8km), created to be undertaken in a single day. Starting and finishing at the village of Goathland, it uses thirteen prominent crosses for their original purpose, as waymarkers.

imagine how reassuring it would have been to see a moorland cross appear through the mist. The spiritual aspect of these moorland crosses was further emphasised by the custom of leaving coins on them – many had an indentation on the top – for needy travellers.

Many stone crosses on the moorland now exist only as empty 'sockets' or just names on old maps. However, at least 30 of the moorland crosses still stand to their full height. Ralph Cross, at 9 feet (2.75m) high on the top of Blakey Ridge, is also known as Young Ralph. It has been a familiar landmark for centuries, since it marks a meeting of important tracks. Now it can be seen by motorists driving between Castleton and Hutton-le-Hole. Close by are two more crosses: 'Old Ralph' is a mere 4 feet (1.2m) high, while 'Fat Betty' comprises a rounded stone 'head' on a square stone 'body'.

The oldest cross still standing on the moors is reckoned to be Lilla Cross, off the Whitby–Pickering road at Ellerbeck Bridge. Possibly of 10th-century origin, it is said to mark the final resting place of Lilla, a minister to King Edwin, whose kingdom encompassed the Yorkshire Wolds. Lilla saved the life of his king by falling on to the sword of an assassin, but inevitably died in the process. King Edwin commemorated this selfless act with the cross you can still see today.

WHEELDALE

The Romans made few incursions into what we now know as the North York Moors. The inescapable conclusion is that the wastes of what for centuries was known as 'Blackamore' held few attractions for the colonists. However, they may have built a road across the moors to link a settlement at Malton with the signal stations on the coast near Goldsborough and Whitby.

A section of road on Wheeldale Moor, just over a mile (1.6km) in length and known as Wade's Causeway, is reckoned to be the best-preserved Roman road in the country, though doubts have been expressed in recent years about its Roman origins. The road gradually fell into disuse, eventually disappearing beneath the encroaching heather and bracken. It was rediscovered in 1914. It can be reached by driving north from Pickering on an unclassified road. Once past the village of Stape, follow the Wheeldale Road with Cropton Forest on the right and the expanse of Wheeldale Moor to the left. Park your car near to the watersplash at Wheeldale Bridge, and the old Roman road is immediately ahead. The Roman Road over Wheeldale is also signposted from the village of Goathland, west of the A169.

We all learned about the Romans' innovative road-making skills at school, yet this particular road looks a rather rocky thoroughfare. That's because what you can see today is merely the road's foundations, made up of large stones set into gravel. The original road surface would have been much smoother, overlaid with finer aggregate. The road is cambered so that water would drain off to the edges and be carried away in culverts. You can follow the route and decide for yourself whether or not you are walking in the footsteps of those Roman legions.

The Iron Valley of Rosedale

Rosedale is a peaceful valley that pushes northwest into the heart of the North York Moors. Yet little more than a hundred years ago the village of Rosedale Abbey had a population ten times its present size. The reason was the discovery of ironstone in the hills in the mid 1850s. The dramatic remains of the Rosedale East Mines, which opened in 1865, can be seen during much of the walk. The long range of huge arches is the remains of the calcining kilns, where the ironstone was roasted to eliminate the impurities and reduce its weight.

Route Directions

1 From your parking place in the hamlet of Thorgill, continue to walk up the lane, pass a public bridleway sign and then go through a metal gate to a track. Follow the track ahead, going through a wooden gate and beginning to rise. Almost opposite to a farmhouse on the left, go right to cross over a wooden stile beside a gate.

2 Walk down the slope to pass over the stream on a gated footbridge, then turn slightly left to go uphill on the opposite bank beside the trees. Continue through a gate into the field and then continue ahead, going over a stile then through a metal gate into the yard of Craven Garth Farm. Go through another gateway and pass between the buildings to reach Daleside Road, a metalled country lane.

3 Turn right; just before reaching the cottage, turn left up a track by the parish notice board. A little way up the track look for a stile beside the gate to Clough House.

4 Go over the stile and follow the track downhill towards the wood, passing around the garden of Clough House. Continue to reach a stile, where you turn right and follow the waymarked path through the wood to reach a stile on to a road.

5 Turn right and then go left through a gate at a bridleway sign. Go down the grassy path to meet a level track. Turn left. Just before a gate, turn right, following the bridleway sign. Continue downhill to reach a ladder stile, and go straight ahead across the field to reach a gateway on to a road by a bridleway sign.

6 Cross the road and continue ahead. After passing through a gateway, turn right at the footpath sign before the bridge. The track climbs steeply to a road. Turn left along the road to a T-junction.

7 Turn left. Opposite the Bell End Farm sign turn right through a gate, and continue down the field to a stile. The path bends and descends steeply. On reaching a fence, turn sharp right to go over a boardwalk and through a waymarked gate. Follow the path over two stiles. Turn left down the track, which passes though a gateway, and go straight on.

8 Just beyond a gate, go left, following the stream, to cross over footbridge with stiles at each end. Follow the footpath uphill heading towards farm buildings. Follow waymarks through the buildings and up the farm track to reach a lane. Turn right here and go back to your car-parking place.

Route facts

DISTANCE/TIME
3.5 miles (5.7km) 1h30

MAP OS Explorer OL26
North York Moors – Western

START Thorgill, grid ref:
SE 708964. Roadside
parking – please be
considerate.

TRACKS Mostly field paths
and tracks, 11 stiles

GETTING TO THE START
From the A170 between
Pickering and Wombleton,
head north to Rosedale
Abbey. Thorgill is a short
distance northwest.

THE PUB The Milburn Arms
Hotel, Rosedale Abbey.
Tel: 01751 417541

❶ Suitability: there's a
steep ascent in Point 6 and
a steep decent in Point 7.

■ TOURIST INFORMATION CENTRE

Hutton-le-Hole
Ryedale Folk Museum.
Tel: 01751 417367

■ PLACES OF INTEREST

There will be an admission charge at the places of interest unless otherwise stated.

Cawthorne
Remains of Roman camp on road between Cropton and Newton-on-Rawcliffe. Free.

Nunnington Hall
Nunnington.
Tel: 01439 748283

Ryedale Folk Museum
Hutton-le-Hole.
Tel: 01751 417367; www.ryedalefolkmuseum.co.uk

■ SHOPPING

MARKET
Kirkbymoorside
Open-air market, Wed.

LOCAL SPECIALITIES
Ceramics
James Brooke, The Pottery, Appleton-le-Moors.
Tel: 01751 417514

Glass
Gillies Jones Glass Design,
The Old Forge,
Rosedale Abbey.
Tel: 01751 417550;
www.gilliesjonesglass.co.uk

■ SPORTS & ACTIVITIES

HORSE-RIDING
Newtondale Horse Trail
35 traffic-free miles (56km).
Guidebook from North York Moors National Park Authority

Sinnington
Friars Hill Riding Stables.
Tel: 01751 432758;
www.friarshillstables.co.uk

MOUNTAIN BIKING AND CYCLE HIRE
Cropton
Donald Wilkie Bike Hire,
Keldy Forest Cabins, Cropton Forest. Tel: 01751 417510 (summer only).
North York Moors Mountain Bike Routes.
www.muddybums.org.uk

WATERSPORTS
Sutherland Lodge Activity Centre, Cropton.
Tel: 01751 417228
Canoeing.

■ ANNUAL EVENTS & CUSTOMS

Hutton-le-Hole
World Merrills Championships, (board game) Sep.

Farndale
Farndale Show, Aug.

Rosedale
Rosedale Show, Aug.

Ryedale
Ryedale Show, Kirkbymoorside, Jul.

FARNDALE

Tea Rooms

Hovingham Bakery Spa Tearoom

Brookside, Hovingham, YO62 4LG. Tel: 01653 628898
The Bakery provides delicious fresh bread and cakes to locals and visitors, and serves them in its little tea room by the beck – you can sit outside on summer days. The hearty sandwiches are a meal in themselves, and there are excellent cream teas – the fruit scones are a particular favourite.

Nunnington Hall

Nunnington, YO62 5UY. Tel: 01439 748283; www.nationaltrust.org.uk
As you'd expect from the National Trust, the food is top-notch. Cream teas, cakes (try the special Nunnington Fruit Loaf) and light lunches will tempt you. If you're there later in the season, you'll find old apple varieties from the orchard used in pies, flans, crumbles, soups and chutneys – worth making a special autumn journey for!

Abbey Tea Rooms and Store

Rosedale Abbey, YO18 8SA. Tel: 01751 417475
As well as plain, fruit and cheese scones, you can find cherry scones, scones made with treacle, scones made with blueberries and ginger... and you can spread them with blueberry and lavender jam. If you're more peckish, try the Yorkshire Ham afternoon tea.

Lastingham Grange

Lastingham, YO62 6TH. Tel: 01751 417345; www.lastinghamgrange.com
Take tea in this elegant hotel on the hillside on the edge of Lastingham. The traditional afternoon teas are served in the drawing room, where you can loll on comfy chintz sofas in front of the fire – it's almost like visiting the gracious home of a wealthy great-aunt.

Pubs

The Lion Inn

Blakey Ridge, Kirkbymoorside, YO62 7LQ. Tel: 01751 417320; www.lionblakey.co.uk
The Lion is set on the high moors at the heart of the National Park. Expect to rub shoulders with walkers and mountain-bikers, as well as lovers of real ale and those who enjoy good, well-cooked and substantial meals, eaten either in the restaurant or the bar. You're sure of a warm welcome, whatever the weather at this exposed spot.

The New Inn

Cropton, Nr. Pickering, YO18 8HH. Tel: 01751 417330; www.croptonbrewery.com
The Cropton micro-brewery produces fine ales that you can sample in its own pub, the New Inn. There is good food available, too, using local ingredients, including fish from Whitby. You can eat either in the cosy bar or in the elegant restaurant.

The Star Inn

Harome, Nr Helmsley, YO62 5JE. Tel: 01439 770397; www.thestaratharome.co.uk
While you're welcome to drop in for a drink (hand-pulled beers, a good selection of wines) it's the Michelin-rated food that is the draw. It is superb, though not cheap. There's a shop selling home-made delicacies.

The George and Dragon

Market Place, Kirkbymoorside, YO62 6AA. Tel: 01751 433334; www.georgeanddragon.net
The George caters for visitors and locals, who enjoy its historic atmosphere. There's real ale on tap and more than 50 types of whisky. The good food is available either in the restaurant or bistro, or by the fire in the bar. The menu is strong on seafood and fish.

Eastern Moors & Coast

BROMPTON ■ GOATHLAND ■ WALK 7 ■ HACKNESS

HOLE OF HORCUM ■ LEVISHAM AND LOCKTON

NORTH YORKSHIRE MOORS RAILWAY ■ PICKERING ■ RAVENSCAR

ROBIN HOOD'S BAY ■ WALKS 8, 9 & 10 ■ SCARBOROUGH

SLEIGHTS ■ THORNTON LE DALE ■ CYCLE RIDES 2 & 3

The eastern moors is the triangle formed between Whitby, Scarborough and Pickering. The coastline provides spectacular cliffs, hidden coves, sandy beaches and fascinating rock formations. To preserve the area's unique character, many miles have been declared designated Heritage Coast. Robin Hood's Bay is one of the loveliest fishing villages in the country, whilst Scarborough is Yorkshire's premier seaside resort.

7 Walk start point

2 Cycle start point

ROBIN HOOD'S BAY

Unmissable attractions

Explore Levisham and Lockton, a pair of delectable moorland villages and discover one of the earliest sites for Iron Age smelting on the nearby moors...explore the beautiful Forge Valley, which is a haven for wildlife...negotiate around the Hole of Horcum, sometimes known as the Devil's Punchbowl, a huge natural amphitheatre scooped out of Levisham Moor...ride high on the restored North Yorkshire Moors Railway, steam-hauled trains taking you deep into the moors...explore the charming resort of Robin Hood's Bay...treat yourself to a day out at Scarborough, one of Britain's oldest medicinal spas and bucket-and-spade seaside resorts.

1 Hole of Horcum
Otherwise known as the Devil's Punchbowl, this deep-sided, natural hollow offers plenty of good opportunities for walks.

2 Robin Hood's Bay
With its cobbled streets and tiny cottages, Robin Hood's Bay, is one of the loveliest fishing villages.

3 Scarborough rock pools
These young holiday-makers are well equipped to explore the fascinating rock pools exposed at low tide in Scarborough.

4 Quoits in Goathland
The game of quoits is played in many moorland villages. The object is to throw a heavy iron quoit over the peg, a metal pin, but there's much more to it than that, as you'll discover if you watch seasoned players, like these in Goathland.

5 North Yorkshire Moors Railway
During the summer months steam trains haul their passengers through some of the finest scenery of the North York Moors.

BROMPTON MAP REF SE9482

Motorists on the A170 tend to drive straight through Brompton in their haste to get to the Yorkshire coast. The pretty little village is set around a small lake, into which the church doors were thrown during the Civil War; they were later recovered and re-hung. The poet William Wordsworth took the time to get to know the village, for he courted Mary Hutchinson, a local girl who lived at Gallows Hill Farm. When they married, in 1802, it was in Brompton's 14th-century church. The wedding ceremony was recorded in her diary by his sister Dorothy; she even joined the happy couple on their honeymoon in Grasmere, in the Lake District.

The village has a unique (though sadly little-known) place in the history of aeronautics. Everybody knows it was Wilbur and Orville Wright who made the first manned flight, in their flimsy craft, Kittyhawk. Yet a remarkable 50 years before that memorable occasion, an unsung squire of Brompton Hall quietly set about building a flying machine.

Brompton Hall (now a school and not open to the public) had been the home of the Cayley family since Stuart times, and Sir George Cayley (1771–1857) developed an unquenchable scientific curiosity. This was an age when enthusiastic amateurs, especially those blessed with private incomes, could indulge their whims in the arts and sciences. Sir George, however, was no mere dabbler; his inventions included caterpillar tracks and a new form of artificial limb, prompted by an accident to one of his estate workers. Seeing how the River Derwent regularly flooded the flat countryside, to the chagrin of local farmers, he designed and constructed a sea cut to divert flood waters straight into the North Sea near Scarborough.

But the prospect of flight remained Sir George's passion. Even before the 18th century was out he was designing gliders – continuing to refine the craft's aerodynamics until he had a controllable machine that could carry a man. He had already experimented with propellers, abandoning them merely because the internal combustion engine was not even on the horizon. His various experiments proved that a contoured wing could provide much greater lift than a wing with a flat profile.

Though an inscription in the church porch acknowledges Sir George as the 'Father of Aeronautics', his pioneering efforts are largely overlooked. Facing the main road through the village is the six-sided building, the summerhouse, now boarded up, unfortunately, where Sir George worked on his flying machines.

■ Insight

A RELUCTANT VOLUNTEER

Taking to heart the notion 'Why have a dog and bark yourself?', Sir George Cayley volunteered his understandably reluctant coachman to make the first manned flight. On a still day in 1853 the glider made a short 55-yard (50m) hop across Brompton Dale. The coachman, relieved to have survived unscathed, but unwilling to entertain thoughts of another death-defying flight, resigned on the spot, telling Sir George that he was paid to drive, not to fly.

GOATHLAND MAP REF NZ8301

This pleasant village has achieved fame by proxy as the location for the popular television series *Heartbeat*. On the small screen Goathland is transformed into fictional Aidensfield, where PC Rob Walker (actor Jonathan Kerrigan) treads his rural beat. Episodes were filmed throughout the moors, but the village of Goathland will be especially familiar to viewers; there is no need to search for locations the cameras have blessed.

Goathland was a popular destination for visitors long before the television series began, and though by no means the prettiest village on the moors, it is certainly well worth visiting in its own right. The broad grass verges, closely cropped by sheep, lead directly on to the heather and bracken of the moors. The village also makes an excellent centre for exploring the surrounding moorland and the stretch of Roman road known as Wade's Causeway. Fame brings its own problems, however, and Goathland does get very busy on Bank Holidays.

Black-faced moorland sheep are everywhere, local farmers enjoy grazing rights throughout the village, so the sheep roam where they will. They keep the grass closely cropped, but have only the most rudimentary road sense.

A brief investigation of the village and its surroundings will reveal a number of delightful waterfalls. The best known is the 70-foot (21m) Mallyan Spout, easily reached via a footpath adjacent to the Mallyan Spout Hotel. The hotel's Victorian architecture is a reminder that the first influx of visitors came with the building of the railway in the 1830s.

■ Visit

THE COLOURFUL MOORS

Leave Goathland in any direction and you will soon find yourself on expansive heather moorland. Though blackened in winter (hence the old name for the moors: 'Blackamore') the heather bursts into life during July, August and September, when miles of tiny flowers paint the uplands in glorious purple. The bell heather has deep purple flowers, while those of the cross-leaved heather have a pinker hue. The scene is made even more colourful during late summer by the blue-black bilberries and the rich brown bracken.

Before that, the village's moorland setting kept it in relative isolation. Goathland's church, just a century old, but on a site of Christian worship for a thousand years, was furnished by Robert Thompson of Kilburn. Look for the little carved mice that were the craftsman's trademark. Near the church is a pinfold, a small, square paddock enclosed by stone walls, where stray beasts could be corralled until claimed by their owners.

Goathland was one of the stations on the main Whitby–Pickering line, a status it retains now that the once-defunct line has a new lease of life as the North Yorkshire Moors Railway. The steepest section of the line was known as the Beck Hole Incline, and it was so steep that the earliest carriages had to be hauled up and down by using a system of counter-balanced weights: a very hazardous procedure. Though tiny and unspoilt today, Beck Hole was briefly, during the middle of the last century, a busy centre of ironstone mining.

Moorland around Goathland and Mallyan Spout

A walk from the popular moorland village of Goathland, also used as the fictitious
village of Aidensfield for the television series *Heartbeat*, through shady woodland
and over the moors. The walk begins with a visit to the impressive 70-foot (21m)
Mallyan Spout waterfall. In dry weather only a trickle of water may fall into the
stream below, but after rain it can become an impressive torrent. After you have
crossed the ford and turned on to the moorland by Hunt House you might find
yourself accompanied by the the sudden flutter of red grouse rising from their
nest sites on the heather moorland.

Route Directions

1 From opposite the church go through the kissing gate to the right of the Mallyan Spout Hotel, signed 'Mallyan Spout'. Follow the path ahead to a streamside signpost and turn left. Continue ahead to pass the waterfall (take care after heavy rain). Next, follow the footpath signs, to cross over two footbridges, over a stile and up steps. Continue by the stream, then ascend to a stile on to a road beside a bridge.

2 Turn left along the road and then climb the hill. Where the road bends left, go right along a bridleway through a gate. Turn left down a path to go over a bridge, then ahead by the buildings, through a gate and across the field.

3 Part-way across the field, go through a gate to the right into woodland. Ascend a stony track, go through a wooden gate then left to another gate on the edge of the wood. Ignoring the gate, turn right up the field, before going left at the top through a gateway. Continue ahead with a wall on your right-hand side, and then go through a waymarked gateway in the wall and up the field, to emerge through a gate on to a metalled lane.

4 Turn left along the lane, go through a gate and follow the 'Roman Road' sign. Next, go through another gate, still following the public bridleway signs as you join a green lane. Continue ahead through a small handgate, to descend to another gate and then on until you reach a ford.

5 Cross over the ford and keep ahead along the track, eventually to reach a road by a bungalow. Turn right up the road and then go left by a wooden garage to continue along a green track which goes up the hillside.

6 At a crossing track, go straight ahead, passsing a small cairn and bending left along the heathery ridge. The obvious path is marked by a series of cairns. Eventually, take a left fork to go down a shallow gill and join a clear track. Goathland church soon comes into sight. Pass a bridleway sign and descend to the road near to the church. The Goathland Hotel can be found on the main street.

Route facts

DISTANCE/TIME
4.5 miles (7.2km) 2h

MAP OS Explorer OL27 North York Moors – Eastern

START The easiest parking is at the west end of the village near the church. West end of Goathland village, near church, grid ref: NZ 827007

TRACKS Streamside tracks, field and moorland paths, 2 stiles

GETTING TO THE START
Goathland is 8 miles (12.9km) southwest of Whitby. It lies just 2 miles (3.2km) west of the A169 Whitby to Malton road and can also be reached using the North Yorkshire Moors Railway from Grosmont or Pickering.

THE PUB The Goathland Hotel, Goathland. Tel: 01947 896203

❶ The initial riverside path to Mallyan Spout is slippery.

HACKNESS   MAP REF SE9790

Steep-sided, wooded valleys fan out from the lovely village of Hackness, which was established at the point where Lowdale Beck meets the River Derwent. It's hard to believe that this secluded spot is only 3 miles (4.8km) from the outskirts of Scarborough. St Hilda, Abbess of Whitby Abbey, established a nunnery here in AD 680, with Abbess Œdilburga; two centuries later Danish invaders razed it to the ground. The community rose again in the 11th century, finally to disappear in 1539 on the orders of Henry VIII.

Hackness Hall (not open to the public), a handsome Georgian house built in 1791 by lord of the manor Sir John Vanden Bempole Johnstone, occupies the site where the nunnery once stood. The only major evidence of that community is the lake, which may have served as a fishery. A more tangible relic, a fragment of an Anglo-Saxon cross, is displayed inside St Peter's Church. Inscriptions, in English, Latin and runic characters, offer up praise to Abbess Œdilburga and prayers for the nuns' own safety. When the cross was carved, possibly in the ninth century, the nuns may have been aware of the cruel fate that awaited them at the hands of marauding Danes.

While Hackness hides in its valley, you can enjoy panoramic views by taking the minor roads to the hilltop villages of Broxa and Silpho. Immediately to the south of Hackness is the Forge Valley, a beautiful, wooded dale created at the end of the Ice Age by glacial meltwater. The River Derwent was diverted from its original direct route, east to the sea at Scalby, to flow south into the Humber.

Forge Valley takes its name from the iron forges, thought to have been worked by the monks of Rievaulx Abbey in the 14th century, which were fuelled by timber felled from this ancient woodland. Today the Forge Valley is a beauty spot and a haven for wildlife. The woods on either side of the river feature native species, including oak, ash, elm and willow, as a pleasant contrast to the regimented conifer plantations that blight rather too many hillsides. Woodpeckers drum insistently; wagtails search for food along the riverbank; tiny warblers fill the woods with song each summer. The walking is excellent at any season of the year. The popularity of the Forge Valley is emphasised by the provision of car parks and picnic sites.

■ Insight

THE GHOST OF HACKNESS

The ghost of Hackness was the invention of an 18th-century vicar's daughter when she found herself a little short of money. She reported seeing a spectral figure that intimated a sum of £50 would allow his soul to be put at rest!

■ Insight

SALT

Since Anglo-Saxon times salt had been valued for its use in curing meat and fish; it was so valuable that a special tax was levied on it. The River Tees, to the north of the National Park, was the site of important salt pans. Tidal waters were evaporated to leave their salt solution, and salt roads – known as saltersgates – led towards Rievaulx, Old Byland and other monastic communities in the north.

Follow the road southwards through woodlands to emerge at the villages of West and East Ayton, sitting astride both the River Derwent and the main A170. At this point the River Derwent is a mere 4 miles (6.4km) from the seaside resort of Scarborough, yet it still has many miles to flow before it reaches the sea at the mouth of the Humber. The river bridge was constructed in 1775, from stone salvaged from the 14th-century castle that once stood near by. Built as a pele tower, a design more commonly found further north, Ayton Castle survives as a ruin.

HOLE OF HORCUM

MAP REF SE8594

This remarkable landform, sometimes known as the Devil's Punchbowl, is a huge natural amphitheatre seemingly scooped out of Levisham Moor. The valley bottom is primarily pastureland, whilst the steep slopes support woods and moorland. Motorists on the A169 Pickering–Whitby road skirt the rim of the Hole of Horcum, and so many stop to gaze in wonderment, and follow some of the good paths in the area, that a large car park has been provided.

Many stories account for the origin of the Hole of Horcum; take your pick between the factual and the fanciful. Legend tells that Wade, a local giant, scooped up a handful of earth to throw at his wife, Bell, thus creating the huge landform. Apparently, he missed her and the clod of earth landed to form Blakey Topping, little more than a mile (1.6km) away. To judge from the plethora of folk tales, Wade and his wife spent much of

■ Visit

A SMUGGLERS' TALE

The smuggling of untaxed salt led to a tragedy. An excise man arrived incognito at the Saltersgate Inn, hoping to catch the smugglers 'red-handed'. When his motives were discovered he was quickly murdered and his body hidden behind the fireplace. From that day, almost 200 years ago, the turf fire has never been allowed to go out. It's a nice story; you can still sit by the fire today and decide for yourself whether it's true. Or you can just take it with a pinch of salt...

their time tossing missiles at one another. But the origin of the Hole of Horcum is more prosaic, scoured over millennia by glacial meltwater.

Just beyond a steep hairpin bend is the Saltersgate Inn, one of the many solitary inns in the National Park. They were generally sited on junctions of well-used tracks, catering for people on the move, as, indeed, they still do today. But instead of holiday-makers, those who stood at the bar of the Saltersgate Inn were more likely to have been hauliers leading trains of heavily laden packhorses across the moors, as the inn lies on an old salt road linking the port of Whitby with the market town of Pickering. Later it catered for stagecoach traffic, and was the site of a tollbooth when the road became a turnpike. It is regularly cut off by snow. Photographs displayed in the bar show the pub almost buried beneath drifts. In less inclement weather it's a convenient port of call after walking around the Hole Horcum.

COATHLAND

GOATHLAND STATION SIGNAL BO

LEVISHAM & LOCKTON

MAP REFS SE8390/SE8489

Levisham and Lockton are a pair of delectable villages lying off the A169, about 5 miles (8km) north of Pickering. Until 1938 the most prominent feature of Lockton's squat church was an ash tree growing out of the top of the square tower. It was removed and replanted in the churchyard, but it failed to thrive. Apart from that, the village has a youth hostel, a duck pond (sadly, few other village ponds in the National Park have survived intact) and limestone cottages set back from wide grass verges.

Neighbouring Levisham is just a mile (1.6km) away, but it is a long mile if you happen to be walking – the villages are divided by a deep gorge. At the bottom, close to Levisham Beck, is a converted watermill and the ruins of St Mary's Church. Though it was built in this isolated spot to be equidistant from both villages, the church can hardly be said to be convenient for either.

Houses, and the Horseshoe Inn, surround a large village green. Pass the pub to join a single track road, with long views along well-wooded Newton Dale. Keep ahead down the road to arrive at Levisham Station, one of the stops for steam trains on the preserved line between Grosmont and Pickering, where the public road ends.

THE NORTH YORKSHIRE MOORS RAILWAY

The North Yorkshire Moors Railway is a remarkable success story. No visit to the moors would be complete without a trip along this most scenic of lines.

Today the line is purely recreational, but it was commerce and industry that provided the original spur for the line to be built. Two centuries ago Whitby was one of the most important ports in the country. By the early 1800s, however, the town's traditional industries – whaling, ship building and alum mining – were in decline and Whitby's traders decided that the town needed to improve the communications over land.

In 1831, George Stephenson arrived fresh from his engineering triumphs on the Stockton and Darlington Railway and surveyed the terrain between Whitby and Pickering. His recommendation was for a railway line on which the carriages would be horse-drawn.

A veritable army of navvies was hired in 1833 to drive the line over the moors. Armed only with pick and shovel they tackled the rough terrain. The line from Whitby to Pickering was opened, with the usual fanfare, in 1836, when a trainload of dignitaries was pulled along the track at a sedate 10 miles per hour.

The line revitalised the area; a variety of industries, such as ironstone mining, sprang up once a regular train service had been established. A few years later it was converted to carry steam engines; the first one chugged noisily into Whitby in 1847. The rather troublesome Beck Hole Incline was bypassed by blasting a new route between Beck Hole and Goathland. By the time a new century dawned the moors and coast were well served with rail links; the trains not only transported goods, they also began to bring visitors from the crowded cities to enjoy the moorland landscape.

■ Insight

THE BECK HOLE INCLINE
The section of the original line of the North Yorkshire Railway between Beck Hole and Goathland (bypassed in 1865) consisted of a 1-in-10 incline. Coaches had to be winched up and down with an imaginative arrangement of counterbalanced weights. Primitive though it was, the moorland railway was immediately hailed as a wonder of engineering.

■ Insight

DETERMINED ENTHUSIASTS
Wheb Beeching closed the railway line between Pickering and Grosmont in 1965, the story might have ended there, except that a group of enthusiasts, convinced that the line still had a viable future, formed themselves into the North Yorkshire Moors Railway Preservation Society. They raised enough money to buy the trackbed from British Rail and then restored the line and the stations along it. After plenty of hard work, the line was partially reopened in 1969 and from end to end in 1973. Today, it is a popular attraction with tourists and railway enthusiasts.

In 1965, as a result of the Beeching Reports, nearly 130 years of rail services came to a halt. The Esk Valley line was reprieved, but the section of railway line between Pickering and Grosmont was unceremoniously closed. Eight years of careful restoration and hard work later the line was reopened by the North Yorkshire Moors Railway Preservation Society. More than just another line run by enthusiasts, the North Yorkshire Moors Railway operates a full timetable from March to October.

The 18-mile (29km) rail journey takes visitors into the very heart of the moors. Today, more than 300,000 passenger journeys are taken every year, making the railway the biggest single attraction within the North York Moors National Park. Many travellers board the train at Pickering Station, which dates from 1845 and the advent of steam-hauled trains. Railway enthusiasts will be happy to know that, a century and a half later, the age of steam hasn't disappeared. The line climbs into the spectacular, steep-sided, wooded gorge of Newton Dale, before arriving at Levisham Station. Trains also call at Newtondale Halt, the starting point for a number of waymarked walks.

The next stop is Goathland, which is a favourite destination for visitors, whether travelling by car or rail. With its waterfalls, Rail Trail and delightful moorland setting, the village is well worth exploring. The northern terminus of the North Yorkshire Moors Railway is Grosmont, where travellers can join the main Northern Spirit line between Middlesbrough and Whitby.

PICKERING   MAP REF SE7984

The market town of Pickering lies just to the south of the National Park. Overlooking the market place is the large parish church dedicated to Saints Peter and Paul. Hemmed in by houses and shops, the building is approached by gates (streets) and ginnels (alleys). Inside are fine 15th-century frescoes, illustrating scenes from the lives of saints and martyrs. St George slays a dragon; Thomas Becket expires in the cathedral; St Edmund raises his eyes towards heaven as arrows fired by Vikings pierce his flesh.

After the Norman Conquest, King William created outposts in the north to establish order and quell uprisings; Pickering was one of these strategic sites. The first castle was built to a basic motte and bailey design; by the 12th century the wooden keep and outer palisade had been rebuilt in stone. It was besieged by Robert the Bruce on one of his incursions south of the border. When the Scots inflicted a heavy defeat on the army led by Edward II in 1322, the king found shelter here.

The castle saw no further military action, and was used by a succession of monarchs as a hunting lodge. Some parts of the old forest are still royal properties, but Pickering Castle is now in the hands of English Heritage.

Beck Isle Museum, housed in a fine Regency building close to Pickering Beck, offers fascinating glimpses into the more recent past. Successive rooms are devoted to different aspects of bygone life in town and country; you can visit the cobblers, gents' outfitters, kitchen, barber's shop and even the bar of a public house. Outbuildings house a blacksmith's forge, wheelwright and a collection of old farming implements.

RAVENSCAR   MAP REF NZ9801

Great things were planned for Ravenscar. A developer called John Septimus Bland decided to build a holiday resort that he thought would rival Whitby and Scarborough. A station was built, Bland laid out the town's network of roads and began to build shops and houses. But Bland's company went bankrupt, and work stopped. Despite the panoramic sea views, this exposed site was clearly unsuitable for such a development. It is geologically unstable, and visitors would have been faced with an awkward descent to the stony beach far below.

■ Visit

MEDIEVAL FRESCOES

The wall paintings in Pickering's church have had a chequered history. They were probably first hidden from view during a bout of puritanical zeal after the Reformation, when such images were considered idolatrous. Rediscovered in 1851, they were almost immediately concealed once again beneath layers of whitewash on the directions of a vicar who shared this puritanical outlook. However, the frescoes were revealed once again in 1878, and are now recognised as some of the best medieval church paintings to be seen in the country.

■ Visit/Activity

RAVENSCAR'S COASTLINE

The fault-line that runs along the coast between Boulby and Scarborough is most clearly visible at Ravenscar. At low tide the rocky shoreline is revealed as a series of concentric curves, formed from layers of hard and soft rock, eroded by the waves over millions of years. This is excellent walking country, on either the beach or cliff-top. The Cleveland Way and the trackbed of the old Whitby–Scarborough railway, open to walkers and cyclists, are near by. Ravenscar is also the finish to the 42-mile (67.2km) hike across the moors from Osmotherley known as the Lyke Wake Walk.

You can see Ravenscar's street layout today, though grass is growing where the buildings ought to have been. When the Raven Hall Hotel was built in 1774, it was simply Raven Hall. The hotel was to have been the centrepiece of the resort; now it stands alone, its mock battlements a landmark for miles around.

The Romans built a signal station here; its foundations and an inscribed stone (on display in Whitby's Pannett Park Museum) were found when Raven Hall's own foundations were being laid. The signal station relayed warnings of Anglo-Saxon invaders to military bases.

This part of the coastline (in the care of the National Trust, visit their Coastal Centre in Ravenscar) was exploited in the 17th century for alum, used in dyeing to fix colours permanently. Remains of the quarries and buildings can be found near Ravenscar.

ROBIN HOOD'S BAY

MAP REF NZ9505

Robin Hood's Bay vies with Staithes for the title of the prettiest fishing village on Yorkshire's coastline. Both communities have to juggle the conflicting demands of tourism with the needs of local people. To visit Robin Hood's Bay be sure to leave your car at the top of the hill, where there are two large car parks. The road down to the beach is a cul-de-sac and visitors' cars are barred.

Apart from the access road, the houses – which cling precariously to the side of the cliff – are reached by narrow alleyways and steps. The result is a jumble of whitewashed cottages and red-tiled roofs leading down the main street and almost into the sea. An old story tells of a ship which at high tide came so close to shore that its bowsprit knocked out the window of a pub!

There is no harbour. Where once there were more than a hundred fishing boats, there are now just a handful, and they are launched down a slipway. Many of the old fishermen's cottages are now holiday homes. There is a good stretch of sandy beach and a rocky foreshore; children love to investigate the little rock pools left in these scars by the receding tide. Take care; it is easy to get cut off by the tide when it starts coming in again.

Robin Hood's Bay has had its share of storms, their effects exacerbated by the softness of the rock that forms the cliffs. A sea wall helps to blunt the worst of the buffeting, though every winter still brings memorable storms.

The only community of any size between Whitby and Scarborough, the relative isolation of Robin Hood's Bay helped to make it a haunt of smugglers. It used to be said that a boat-load of contraband could be beached, and the load transferred to the top of the village through a maze of secret passages between the tightly packed houses, all without seeing the light of day.

You can walk at low tide along the beach (keep an eye out for the incoming tide) to Ravenscar, high on its cliff-top to the south, or along a fascinating section of the Cleveland Way. On your way, about a mile (1.6km) from Robin Hood's Bay, is Boggle Hole, a little wooded cove. An old water mill, once powered by Mill Beck, is now a youth hostel conveniently situated for Cleveland Wayfarers.

Cleveland Way and Robin Hood's Bay

A walk through fields and along the coastal Cleveland Way from Robin Hood's Bay and back. On the coastal path you will notice how the sea is encroaching on the land: the loss here is said to be 6 inches (15cm) every two years.

Route Directions

1 From the lower car park opposite The Victoria Hotel, turn left up the hill and, where the road bends round to the left, take a signed footpath to the right over a stile. Walk up the fields over three stiles to a metalled lane.

2 Turn right. Go left through a signed metal gate. At the end of the field the path bends right to a gate in the hedge on your left. Continue down the next field with a stone wall on your left. Again, go right at the end of the field and over a stile into a green lane.

3 Cross over the green lane to another waymarked stile and continue along the field edge with a wall on your right. At the end of the field go over a stile on your right and then make for a waymarked gate diagonally left.

4 Walk towards the Bottom House Farm, go through a gate and then take the waymarked track round the right of the buildings to reach another gate, then to a waymarked opening beside a metal gate. Continue with a stone wall on your right, go through another gate and on to a track that eventually bends left to reach a waymarked stile.

5 Continue to another stile, which leads to a derelict footbridge over a narrow beck. At a T-junction by a wooden electricity pylon, veer right and take a path to the right of the bank. After 50yds (46m), look for a signpost for Hawsker in woodland. Walk to the signpost then follow it right. As the hedge to your right curves left, go through a gap on the right and over a signed stile, walking straight ahead through the field to an opening by the main road.

6 Go right and right again, following the footpath sign, up the metalled lane towards two holiday parks. Pass Seaview Caravan Park, cross the former railway track and continue along the metalled lane, which bends right, goes downhill, crosses a stream and ascends to the Northcliffe holiday park.

7 Follow the footpath sign right, then go left and follow the metalled track down through the caravans, eventually leaving the track to go left to a waymarked path. Follow the path towards the coastline, to reach a signpost.

8 Turn right along the Cleveland Way for 2.5 miles (4km) alongside eroded shaly

Route facts

DISTANCE/TIME
5.5 miles (8.8km) 2h30

MAP OS Explorer OL27 North York Moors – Eastern

START There are two main car parks, both off to the right of the B road in the upper part of the village. The lower streets are access only. Car park at top of hill by the old railway station, Robin Hood's Bay, grid ref: NZ 950055.

TRACKS Field and coastal paths, a little road walking, 14 stiles

GETTING TO THE START The old smugglers' village at Robin Hood's Bay huddles in a coastal hollow at the end of the B1447. It can be accessed from High Hawsker on the A171 Whitby to Scarborough road.

THE PUB The Victoria Hotel, Robin Hood's Bay. Tel: 01947 880205

❶ Take care on the road at the beginning of the walk. Keep well away from the friable cliff edges.

cliffs. At Rocket Post Field there's a minor waymarked diversion across fields to the right, caused by the cliff path collapsing into the sea. On the approach to Robin Hood's Bay go left through a gate and continue past houses to reach the main road. Turn left here to return to the car park.

Through Scarborough's Raincliffe Woods

Just outside Scarborough, a walk through woodland to the rare remains of a glacial lake. The steep hillside of Raincliffe Woods overlooks a deep valley carved out in the Ice Ages. Although mostly replanted in the 1950s and 60s, the woods in places retain remnants of ancient oak and heather woodland – look out for the heather and bilberry bushes beneath oak trees that will show you where. Throughout the walk you will come upon humps and banks, depressions and pits that show that this hillside has been a hive of human activity in the past. As the path approaches Throxenby Mere it crosses part of a Bronze Age dyke system, while elsewhere are medieval banks and the remains of pits for charcoal burning.

Route Directions

1 From the picnic site, walk on to the road and turn left, downhill. After the woodland ends, pass houses on the right, then opposite a bungalow, No 5, turn right down a track to Thorn Park Farm. Follow the track as it bends left by the farm buildings, then right past a cottage to a metal gate. Continue to follow the track, which bends left then right, then passes through two gateways.

2 Just before the next gateway turn right and walk up the field side to a stile beside a gateway, which takes you on a short path to the road. Turn left. Follow the road to the next car park on the right.

3 Go through the car park towards the gate and uphill on the path ahead. Where the main path bends right, go ahead, more steeply, to reach a crossing, grassy track. Turn left through a gate and follow the path. Where it forks, take the right-hand path.

4 Look out for a path on the left, which immediately bends right over a drainage runnel. The path goes down into a small valley. Turn left, downhill, then follow the path as it bends right again, past an old quarry. The path then descends to Throxenby Mere.

5 Turn right along the edge of the Mere – part of the path is on boardwalks. Just before you reach a picnic place, turn right through an area bare of undergrowth to take a path that goes up steeply until it reaches a grassy track at the top of the hill.

6 Turn right and go through a metal gate, then follow the path for a mile (1.6km), parallel with the wall. It passes through a gateway with a stile by it and finally reaches a gate with a public bridleway sign.

7 Don't go through the gate into fields, but turn right and continue into woodland. Where the main path swings left and another goes right, go ahead, steeply downhill. When the path joins another go left, go down steps and along a boardwalk to meet a crossing path.

8 Turn right and descend to a gate into a car park. Turn left onto the road, and left again to a road junction. Turn right, following the Harwood Dale sign, for Hazelhead picnic site.

Route facts

DISTANCE/TIME
5 miles (8km) 2h

MAP OS Explorer OL27
North York Moors – Eastern

START Hazelhead picnic site on Mowthorpe Road, near road junction, grid ref: SE 984875

TRACKS field tracks, woodland paths, some steep, 2 stiles

GETTING TO THE START
West Ayton is on the A170 around 3 miles (5km) west of Scarborough. Hazelhead picnic site on Mowthorpe Road, near road junction

THE PUB Ox Pasture Hall Country Hotel, Throxenby. Tel: 01723 365295

Early warnings at Fylingdales and Lilla Cross

The past and the future come together on this walk on the North Yorkshire coast. Unlike in most of upland Britain, the most important roads and tracks in the North York Moors follow the ridges between the valleys. The tracks are often marked by standing stones or crosses, many of them of great antiquity. The most impressive and most ancient of the Moor's crosses is Lilla, which commemorates a selfless deed of bravery in AD 626, when Lilla died protecting King Edward of Northumbria from assassination. Dominating the middle section of the walk is the improbably large sandcastle that houses the Fylingdales early warning system. It's heavily fenced and there are forbidding notices, but from a distance it's impressive.

Route Directions

1 Walk up the wide track opposite the approach road. At the point where the track bends round to the right, go left down a signed footpath and descend to cross over a bridge and continue along the green track. Go through a kissing gate and continue up the side of the valley, finally swinging away from the stream and continuing into the forest.

2 On reaching a forest road turn right, passing a flooded quarry on your right. At the next junction of forest roads bear right. After about 0.5 miles (800m), look for a broad ride to the left, with a white bicycle waymark by it.

3 Go up the ride, leaving the forest, and out on to moorland. Continue past the base and shaft of York Cross. Pass a track going left and continue until you reach a waymarked (bridleway) post, where you turn sharp left.

4 Walk along the track, passing Foster Howes, and continue with the fence on your right. Pass Ann's Cross to your right and 0.5 miles (800m) beyond this you'll reach a T-junction, where you turn right and continue along the bridleway.

5 When you reach a crossroads with a signpost, turn right along the track to visit Lilla Cross, which can be seen a little way away. After visiting the cross, return to the crossroads, and then go straight ahead, following the Robin Hood's Bay sign. The path goes parallel with the forest edge.

6 Go right when you reach a post with the number 9 on it. Pass posts 8 and 7, going left when you reach a trail sign.

7 Pass post 6 (by the remains of John Cross) and go through a gate, to continue walking downhill on a track. When you reach a yellow waymarker leave the track and walk down to the left until you get to a waymarked stile near the ruins of a building.

8 Go to the left of the ruined building and make for another stile. Follow the obvious footpath downhill through the bracken, passing two public footpath signs, and climb over another wooden stile to reach the road. Turn left to return to the start.

Route facts

DISTANCE/TIME
7.5 miles (12km) 2h30

MAP OS Explorer OL27 North York Moors – Eastern

START May Beck car park, grid ref: SE 893025

TRACKS Forest tracks and moorland paths, 3 stiles

GETTING TO THE START From Whitby take the A171 south, passing the turn off to Robin Hood's Bay. Turn right at the junction with the B1416. Take the 1st left, a minor road, to May Beck car park.

THE PUB The Birch Hall Inn, Goathland.
Tel: 01947 896245

SCARBOROUGH MAP REF TA0488

The resort of Scarborough can claim to be one of the oldest in the country. Its prosperity can be traced back to the occasion in the year 1620, when a visitor, Mrs Elizabeth Farrow, was drinking a glass of spring water. Finding the water acidic in taste, she came to the natural conclusion that something that tasted so unpleasant must surely have medicinal qualities too.

Promises of miraculous cures have always had willing ears, the more outlandish the better. Scarborough's spring water was said to cure many ills, even hypochondria: surely a rather self-defeating exercise, since hypochondriacs were precisely the sort of people to whom the town extended the warmest welcome. Scarborough's spring water certainly contains Epsom salts and a cocktail of minerals. It was definitely good for one thing – giving the town's economy a much-needed shot in the arm. The taking of the waters was soon put on a more commercial footing. Scarborough became known as a spa town; a name borrowed from the Belgian resort. Scarborough was put firmly on the map as a place where the well-heeled might come to recuperate at leisure. Emboldened by this success, a local doctor started to extol the health-giving properties of sea bathing. One way or another Scarborough's waters were responsible for its success.

The first spa house was built over the original spa well in 1700. However, it was to suffer the fate shared by many other Scarborough buildings, by falling into the sea. Ever more elaborate spa houses were built, each one getting the royal stamp of approval for the water's efficacy. By the time Queen Victoria ascended to the throne, Scarborough was arguably the North's finest resort; many of the town's most distinguished buildings date from Victoria's reign. The Grand Hotel, overlooking the South Bay, seems to sum up the prosperity of Scarborough during the busiest time in its long history.

Scarborough Castle has dominated the town with an air of fortress-like impregnability for the best part of a millennium. Standing proudly on its headland, between the North and South Bays, it enjoys an uninterrupted view over the town and out to sea. Remains of even earlier defences have been unearthed, including an Iron-Age settlement and a Roman signal station.

The Norman edifice we see today can be dated to the year 1136, when William de Gros decided to rebuild in stone an earlier wooden fort. Henry II, concerned that many of his noblemen were growing too powerful, set about destroying their castles. He spared Scarborough Castle, however. Impressed by its air of impregnability, he requisitioned the castle and kept it for himself.

Besieged on a number of occasions, Scarborough Castle was never taken by force, but attacking forces managed to starve the defenders into surrendering. On one occasion, in 1645, Hugh Cholmley's Royalist troops were besieged by John Meldrum's Scottish army and the Great Keep was badly damaged by the Scottish artillery. Unable to hold out any longer, they were allowed to

SCARBOROUGH

surrender with honour intact; those men who could still stand were allowed to march out of the castle. The castle was heavily beseiged again in 1648 when the Parliamentary garrison, discontented because they had not been paid, went over to the King's side; they too were starved into submission.

St Mary's Church also suffered artillery damage at the hands of the Royalists defending the castle, which is still visible. Anne Brontë was visiting Scarborough in 1849 when she succumbed to tuberculosis and died. The author of *The Tenant of Wildfell Hall* is buried in the churchyard.

While many of British resorts have lost out to the ease of foreign travel, Scarborough has enough attractions to keep the most fastidious visitors coming back for more. Cricket lovers eagerly anticipate the Scarborough Festival, traditionally held towards the end of the season. Playwright Sir Alan Ayckbourn keeps faith with local theatre-goers by premiering most of his plays here in his Stephen Joseph Theatre before they are transferred to London's West End. The miniature North Bay Railway runs for just under a mile (1.6km) between Peasholme Park and the Sealife Centre at Scalby Mills where you can see a colourful Caribbean-style coral reef, hundreds of fish, turtles and sharks.

SLEIGHTS MAP REF NZ8607

Sleights straddles the River Esk in a sheltered dip in the landscape, just outside the boundary of the National Park. There are few buildings here to attract the eye, but it is a convenient spot from which to explore the surrounding countryside – whether you head for open moorland, or the more intimate environs of the Esk.

Ruswarp, inside the National Park, between Sleights and the sea, marks the tidal limit of the River Esk. Here, on a quiet stretch of the river, you can hire a dinghy for a leisurely row.

A minor road from Sleights leads to a hamlet that glories in the name of Ugglebarnby. The meaning is 'the farm of old owl beard'; the explanation is less easy to fathom. Continue past Ugglebarnby to arrive in Littlebeck, on a road that snakes through this delightful village. Here you can enjoy fine walks, one along May Beck and the other to the south to see Falling Foss, an exquisite waterfall in a woodland setting.

■ Insight

AN IMPREGNABLE FORTRESS
Scarborough Castle has never been taken by force. When the castle was besieged by the Roundheads in 1645 a deep well provided a good supply of fresh water for the Royalist inhabitants. However, the beleaguered soldiers inside the castle eventually ran out of food, and were reduced to eating rats and deriving what little sustenance was available by boiling up their leather belts and boots.

■ Insight

A MIRACULOUS CURE
Elaborate claims were made for the many ailments which Scarborough's spring waters might cure. Once stomach ache, consumption, rheumatism and fever had been taken care of, the waters would sort out palsy, madness and leprosy.

THORNTON-LE-DALE

MAP REF SE8383

Despite being split in two by the busy A170, Thornton-le-Dale is still said to be one of the prettiest villages in Yorkshire. The thatched cottage beside Dalby Beck must be one of the most photographed buildings in the county, making regular appearances on calendars and biscuit tin lids. The boundary of the National Park makes a little detour to include the village – a good indication that it is worth making a stop here. Try to time your visit outside the busier holiday periods, for Thornton-le-Dale is best explored when the crowds are gone.

The tone is established by the beck; its meandering course through the village is punctuated by a succession of tiny bridges. At the crossroads, in the centre of the village, is a small green where the slender, stepped market cross and a set of wooden stocks still stand. On the opposite side of the road are Lady Lumley's Almshouses, a block of twelve dwellings, built in 1670 and still retaining their original use.

The churchyard is the burial place of Matthew Grimes, who died in 1875 at the grand old age of 96. His claim to fame is that he guarded Napoleon during the emperor's exile on the island of St Helena, and helped to carry his body to the grave. Thornton-le-Dale's churchyard is also the last resting place of Sir Richard Chomley, known as The Great Black Knight of the North. He served at the court of Elizabeth I; his home, Roxby Castle, once stood just to the west of Thornton-le-Dale. His effigy can be seen inside the church.

■ **Insight**

'FLINT JACK'

Sleights was the birthplace, in 1815, of 'Flint Jack', who delighted in fooling those experts who came to the moors in search of antiquities. He established a lucrative sideline by manufacturing his own relics, and offering them to collectors and museums as genuine archaeological finds. His fakes and forgeries were so convincing that even the British Museum was fooled into parting with money.

■ **Insight**

SUPERSTITIONS

Superstitions were rife in rural areas. Charms considered to be lucky included a horseshoe (or stone with a natural hole in it), hung from the door of the house. Picking up a pin, or other piece of metal, would prevent a witch from using it in her spells. The rowan tree was also known as witchwood; carrying a crucifix made of rowan wood was a common way to guard against the 'evil eye'. Of course, those who scoff at such unsophistication should examine their own habits: crossing the fingers, playing 'lucky' lottery numbers...

In Ellerburn, just to the north, is the tiny Church of St Hilda, where you'll find many examples of Viking stone work, including several cross heads and a serpent sculpture.

To explore further afield take the Forest Drive (toll payable) through Dalby Forest, which is easily accessible by driving north from Thornton-le-Dale, where there are numerous walking trails, mountain-bike routes, fishing areas and picnic places, a useful visitor centre and shop.

Dalby Forest

This is a short ride through the forest to seek the wildlife – if you stay quiet and look hard enough, you'll see it in abundance. In quieter corners you may stumble upon the Bambi-like roe deer, but it's bird-life you're more likely to spot. Besides the common blue tits, you're quite likely to see a wading heron, or a tiny warbler such as that summer visitor, the chiffchaff, so called because of its birdsong.

Route Directions

1 The green cycle route begins beyond the trees at the southeast end of the large Adderstone Field (the furthest from the visitor centre). Here you turn left along a narrow slightly downhill track. Though still easy, it's the most difficult section of the route – use gentle braking if you're a little unsure. Ignore the two lesser, unsigned left fork tracks.

2 Turn right along a much wider forestry track which takes a winding course round the afforested valley of Worry Gill. Where the more demanding red route goes off on a rough track to the right, your green route goes straight on, still using a well-graded track.

3 Where a track doubles back, go straight on up a

steady hill before meeting up with the forest drive again. Cross this with care – it can be quite busy on summer weekends – before turning right along it for 200yds (183m). Turn left along a narrow path signed with red and green waymarkers and just before a 30 mile per hour speed limit sign (hope you were not speeding!). If you're early and it's summer, you may be able to dally and eat some of the bilberries that grow beside the path.

4 The path reaches a flinted road at the southeast edge of the forest. Turn right along this, then turn left at the next junction. Looking to your left, you'll see the rougher high pastures of Ebberston Low Moor decline to the greener, more fertile fields of the Vale of Pickering.

5 Turn right just before reaching Givendale Head Farm along a rutted farm track with a grassy island in the middle. Turn right at the next junction (Post B) on a downhill section, followed by an uphill one where you're joined by a farm track coming in from the left.

6 A long hill follows to a wide junction where you go straight on along a tarred lane. A sign tells you that you're now at the head of Flax Dale. Stay with the tarred lane at the next bend and junction. Turn right at the crossroads along a long sandy track (Post A), then turn right again at the next junction. Note the linear earthwork to both left and right – nobody seems to know the exact origins of these.

7 After going straight on at the next junction past a fine stand of Scots pines, you get fine views over the farm pastures of High Rigg to reach Levisham Moor. Here, there's another downhill section followed by an uphill one. Take a right fork at Newclose Rigg. Where the red route goes straight on, your green route veers right along the main track. There's a downhill left curve beyond which you take the upper right fork, which brings the route back to the forest drive opposite Adderstone Field.

Route facts

DISTANCE/TIME 6 miles (9.7km) 2h

MAP OS Explorer OL27 North York Moors Eastern

START Car park at Adderstone Field, Dalby Forest, grid ref: SE 883897

TRACKS forestry roads and a few narrow paths, mostly well graded

GETTING TO THE START From the A170 at Thornton le Dale head north on a minor road signed the Dalby Forest, then turn off right on the Dalby Forest Drive, where you'll come to the tollbooths. Adderstone Field, the start of the ride, lies about 5 miles (8km) beyond the visitor centre.

CYCLE HIRE Cycle Hire Kiosk next to Visitor Centre, Low Dalby. Tel; 01751 460400

THE PUB New Inn, Maltongate, Thornton le Dale. Tel: 01751 474226.

❶ There's a short, rough and slightly downhill section of track at the start. The forest drive road needs to be crossed with care twice.

From Ravenscar to Robin Hood's Bay

The former railway line between Whitby and Scarborough can now be followed, in its entirety, on two wheels. The full distance is 20 miles (32.2km) one way, so this ride picks out probably the finest section, looping around Robin Hood's Bay. It is a little confusing that the name of the bay and the much-photographed village are exactly the same, but the ride gives great views of the former and a chance to visit the latter.

Route Directions

1 Descend the road until it bends sharply right. Turn left, past the National Trust Coastal Centre, and continue on an obvious descending concrete track. A rougher section needs more care, but lasts less than 100yds (91m). Now swing left and go through a gate on to the old railway trackbed and a much easier surface.

2 The track now runs below the scarred face of the alum workings, with some ups and downs that clearly don't match the original rail contours exactly. After this section, take care crossing a steep concrete track that runs down to a farm.

3 Pass under an arched bridge. Note more quarried cliffs up on the left, while looking down to the right – if the tide is not too high – there are extensive rocky platforms in the bay, with conspicuous parallel strata. There's a short cutting and the sea views are hidden by tall gorse and broom, then it becomes more open again as the track swings gradually inland. A tall embankment crosses a steep wooded valley. Go under a bridge and then make a sharp left turn on to a lane.

4 Go up 20yds (18m), then sharp right to continue on the track. Keep right at a fork and the track resumes its steady gentle descent, then starts to turn uphill for the first time on the ride. As you come out into the open after a tunnel of trees, the direct way ahead is again blocked (unless you're Evel Knievel!). Here slant down left, cross a lane, and then climb back up on to the continuing trackbed.

5 Pass a cricket ground, the back of a caravan site, then a farm. Cross the rough farm track and keep straight on ahead, through a gate where the surface changes to tarmac, on the outskirts of Robin Hood's Bay. Go through another gate and drop down to a road. Turn right down this road for 100yds (91m) then go left on a lane signposted to Station Workshops. At the top

of the rise is the old station building and just beyond it a large car park. (It is, of course, possible to descend the road all the way into the village of Robin Hood's Bay, but it's a very steep climb back. An alternative is to lock the bikes at the car park and go down on foot.)

6 Continue alongside the car park, drop down to a road, turn left and almost instantly right (very nearly straight across) on to Mount Pleasant. Follow this to its end then bear left up a short gravelled ride to regain the railway path. Continue for about 0.5 mile (800m). There are good views back now over Robin Hood's Bay to the cliffs near Ravenscar. Look for a National Trust sign for Ness Bay. There is open access on foot so you could leave your bikes and walk down to the headland, a great picnic spot. This makes as good a turn-round point as any, though the track continues into Hawsker and on to Whitby.

Route facts

DISTANCE/TIME 11.25 miles (18.1km) 2h

MAP OS Explorer OL27 North York Moors – Eastern

START Roadside parking on way into Ravenscar, grid ref: NZ 980015

TRACKS Almost entirely on well-surfaced old railway track; short street sections at Ravenscar and Robin Hood's Bay

GETTING TO THE START Turn off the A171, midway between Whitby and Scarborough – signed for Ravenscar. Turn left at a T-junction, then right near an old windmill. The road descends into Ravenscar and there is extensive roadside parking as the descent gets steeper.

THE PUB The Laurel Inn, Robin Hood's Bay. Tel: 01947 880400

❶ Busy roads and car park in Robin Hood's Bay village (possible to turn round before this).

ROBIN HOOD'S BAY

■ TOURIST INFORMATION CENTRES

Pickering
The Ropery.
Tel: 01751 473791
Scarborough
Brunswick Shopping Centre,
Westborough.
Tel: 01723 383636
Harbourside, Sandside.
Tel: 01723 383636 (seasonal)

■ PLACES OF INTEREST

There will be an admission charge at the places of interest unless otherwise stated.
Beck Isle Museum
Bridge Street, Pickering.
Tel: 01751 473653;
www.beckislemuseum.co.uk
Crescent Arts Workshop
The Crescent, Scarborough.
Tel: 01723 351461;
www.crescentarts.co.uk
Free.
National Trust Centre
Ravenscar.
Tel: 01723 870138 or 870423
North Yorkshire Moors Railway
Pickering Station, Pickering.
Tel: 01751 472508;
www.northyorkshiremoorsrailway.com
The Old Coastguard Station Visitor Centre
Robin Hood's Bay.
Tel: 01947 885900
Pickering Castle
Tel: 01751 474989

Robin Hood's Bay Museum
Fisherhead.
The Rotunda Museum
Vernon Road, Scarborough.
www.rotundamuseum.org.uk
Reopening 2007/08 as museum of geology
Scarborough Art Gallery
The Crescent.
Tel: 01723 374753; www.scarboroughmuseums.org.uk
Scarborough Castle
Tel: 01723 372451
Sea Life & Marine Sanctuary
Scalby Mills, Scarborough.
Tel: 01723 376125;
www.sealifeeurope.com
Staintondale Shire Horse Farm
Staintondale.
Tel: 01723 870458;
www.shirehorsefarm.co.uk
Woodend Natural History Museum
The Crescent, Scarborough.
Tel: 01723 367326; www.scarboroughmuseums.org.uk

■ FOR CHILDREN

Staintondale Shire Horse Farm
Staintondale.
Tel: 01723 870458;
www.shirehorsefarm.co.uk

■ SHOPPING

MARKET
Open-air market,Pickering, Mon.
LOCAL SPECIALITIES

Ceramics
Green Man Gallery,
8 Park Street, Pickering.
Tel: 01751 472361
Honey
The Honey Farm, East Ayton.
Tel: 01723 865198
Ice-Cream
Beacon Farm, Beacon Way, Sneaton.
Tel: 01947 605212;
www.beacon-farm.co.uk
Trout
Moorland Trout Farm, Pickering.
Tel: 01751 473101

■ PERFORMING ARTS

Futurist Theatre and Cinema
Foreshore Road, Scarborough.
Tel: 01723 365789;
www.futuristtheatre.co.uk
Spa Entertainment Complex
South Bay, Scarborough.
Tel: 01723 376774;
www.scarboroughspa.co.uk
Spa Theatre
South Bay, Scarborough.
Tel: 01723 357869
Stephen Joseph Theatre
Westborough, Scarborough.
Tel: 01723 370541;
www.sjt.uk.com

■ SPORTS & ACTIVITIES

ANGLING
Sea
Boats for hire at the harbour in South Bay, Scarborough.

Fly

Pickering Trout Lake.
Tel: 01751 474219
The Mere, Scarborough.
Day tickets on site.
Wykeham Trout Lakes
(coarse and trout).
Tel: 07946 534001;
www.dawnay.co.uk

BEACHES

There are sandy beaches
with easy access at Robin
Hood's Bay and Scarborough
(North Bay and South Bay).

CRICKET

Scarborough

North Marine Road,
Tel: 01723 365625

GOLF COURSES

Kirkbymoorside

Kirkbymoorside Golf Club,
Manor Vale.
Tel: 01751 431525

Scarborough

North Cliff Golf Club,
North Cliff Avenue.
Tel: 01723 360786. South Cliff
Golf Club, Deepdale Avenue.
Tel: 01723 365150

CYCLE HIRE

Dalby

Purple Mountain Bike Hire,
The Courtyard, Low Dalby.
Tel 01751 460011;
www.purplemountain.co.uk

HORSE-RIDING

Robin Hood's Bay

Farsyde Stud and Riding
Centre. Tel: 01947 880249;
www.farsydefarmcottages.
co.uk

Snainton

Snainton Riding Centre.
Tel: 01723 859218; www.
snaintonridingcentre.co.uk

Staintondale

Pony Trekking Centre.
Tel: 01723 871846

LLAMA TREKKING

Staintondale

Wellington Lodge Llamas.
Tel: 01723 871234;
www.llamatreks.co.uk

LONG-DISTANCE ROUTES

Moor to Sea

80-mile (129km) cycle route
linking Pickering,
Scarborough and Whitby.
www.moortoseacycle.net

The Rail Trail

A 3.5-mile (5.6km) walk from
Goathland to Grosmont
following the track bed of
George Stephenson's original
railway line.

Scarborough to Whitby
Railway Trail

Route for walkers and
cyclists follows the old
railway line. (Cycle hire at
Hawsker.)

FORESTS

Dalby Forest Drive. Free for
pedestrians, cyclists and
Moorsbus passengers.
Dalby Forest Visitor Centre
and shop.
Tel: 01751 472771

■ ANNUAL EVENTS
& CUSTOMS

Littlebeck

Littlebeck Rose Queen
Ceremony, Aug.

Pickering

Jazz Festival, Jul.
Traction Engine Rally, Aug.

Robin Hood's Bay

Folk Festival, Jun.

Scalby

Scalby Fair, early Jun.

Scarborough

Scarborough Fayre, Jun.
International Music Festival,
Jun.
Scarborough Cricket Festival,
end Aug/Sep.

Thornton-le-Dale

Thornton-le-Dale Show, Aug.

Tea Rooms

The Mallyan Spout Hotel
The Common, Goathland,
YO22 5AN. Tel. 01947 896486;
www.mallyanspout.co.uk
You could bump into the stars
of television's *Heartbeat* while
you have afternoon tea at the
Mallyan Spout. Choose from
scones, delicious cakes and
sandwiches, or a more
substantial meal from the
selection that's served all
day. Relax in the lounge or
enjoy the garden and patio.

Foxcliffe Tea Rooms
Station Square, Ravenscar,
YO13 0LU. Tel: 01723 871028
With twelve sorts of tea and
six coffees, the Foxcliffe
offers a wide choice. Based
in one of the few buildings –
part of the station – that were
erected in what was planned
to be a coastal resort to rival
Scarborough, the café offers
home-baked cakes and hot
food – and spectacular cliff-
top and sea views.

The Old Bakery Tea Rooms
Chapel Street, Robin Hood's
Bay, YO22 4SQ.
Tel: 01947 880709
A lovely, traditional tea room,
situated in the heart of the
village. The bread and cakes
are produced in the attached
bakery. Scones with home-
made preserves are a
favourite, along with the
chocolate and coffee cakes.
There's an enclosed balcony
overlooking the stream – a
good place to rest and watch
the world go by.

Warrington House
Whitbygate, Thornton-le-
Dale, YO18 7RY.
Tel: 01751 475028;
www.warringtonhouse.co.uk
Just a few yards from the
bustling centre of Thornton-
le-Dale, this tea room is the
place to enjoy afternoon tea
with a selection of home-
made cakes and scones, a
ploughman's lunch or
vegetable strudel. There's a
delicious array of puddings
on offer, too,

Pubs

Birch Hall Inn
Beckhole, Goathland,
YO22 5LE. Tel: 01947 896245
The Birch Hall is a bit off the
beaten track, though near
the North Yorkshire Moors
Railway line. But it's worth
persevering to find it, as it's
real gem. There's nothing
flashy about it, but if you like
real local ales properly kept
and served, wholesome food
like tasty pies, substantial
sandwiches and their own
delicious beer cake, this is
the place to come.

Moorcock Inn
Langdale End, Scarborough.
YO13 0BN. Tel: 01723 882268
This remote Moors pub has
a tiled floor and a rather odd
assortment of benches in two
small rooms. However, you're
guaranteed a decent drink,
with a changing selection of
beer from local regional and
micro-breweries. In the
summer, home-cooked food
is available, and you can sit
outside in good weather.

Laurel Inn
New Road, Robin Hood's Bay,
YO22 4SE. Tel: 01947 880400
Near to the bottom of the
winding main street, this pub
has a cosy, traditional
atmosphere, with an open
fire. It offers real ales and
simple but wholesome food –
including tasty thick soups in
the winter.

The New Inn
Moorgate, Thornton-le-Dale,
YO28 7LF. Tel: 01751 474226;
www.the-new-inn.com
This fine Georgian building
at the heart of the village
retains its traditional
atmosphere, with log fires
and hand-pulled beer. There
is a flower-filled patio on
which to enjoy a drink, while
the restaurant offers a wide
range of meals using fresh,
locally sourced ingredients.

■ NORTH YORK MOORS NATIONAL PARK INFORMATION POINTS

North York Moors National Park

The Old Vicarage, Bondgate, Helmsley. Tel: 01439 770657; www.northyorkmoors-npa.gov.uk

Useful Websites

www.north-york-moors.com; www.yorkshirenet.co.uk; www.york-moors.co.uk

■ OTHER INFORMATION

Angling

Numerous opportunities for fishing on farms, lakes and rivers. Permits and licences are available from local tackle shops and TICs.

Coastguard

Dial 999 and ask for the Coastguard Service, which co-ordinates rescue services.

English Heritage

Canada House, 3 Chepstow Street, Manchester. Tel: 0161 242 1400; www.english-heritage.org.uk

English Heritage (Yorkshire)

37 Tanner Row, York. Tel: 01904 601901

Environment Agency

Rivers House, 21 Park Sq South, Leeds. Tel: 0113 2440191

Forest Enterprise

Outgang Road, Pickering. Tel: 01751 472771

Health

Information on health problems is available from NHS Direct. Tel: 0845 4647; www.nhsdirect.nhs.uk

Dental Helpline

Tel: 0845 063 1188

Moorsbus Summer Coach and Minibus

Tel 01439 77065; www.moorsbus.net

The National Trust

Goddards, 27 Tadcaster Road, York. Tel: 01904 702021; www.nationaltrust.org.uk

Parking

Information on parking permits and car parks in the area is available from local TICs.

Places of Interest

There will be an admission charge unless otherwise stated. We give details of just some of the facilities within the area covered by this guide. Further information can be obtained from local TICs or the web.

Yorkshire Tourist Board

312 Tadcaster Road, York. Tel: 01904 707961; www.ytb.org.uk

Yorkshire Wildlife Trust

10 Toft Green, York. Tel: 01904 659570; www.yorkshire-wildlife-trust.org.uk

■ ORDNANCE SURVEY MAPS

ESK DALE & NORTH

Explorer 1:25,000 Outdoor Leisure; sheet 26
Landranger 1:50,000; Sheets 93, 94

WESTERN MOORS

Explorer 1:25,000 Outdoor Leisure; sheet 26
Landranger 1:50,000; Sheets 93, 100

CENTRAL MOORS

Explorer 1:25,000 Outdoor Leisure; sheet 26
Landranger 1:50,000; Sheets 93, 94,100

EASTERN MOORS & COAST

Explorer 1:25,000 Outdoor Leisure; sheet 27
Landranger 1:50,000; Sheets 94, 100, 101

The National Grid system covers Great Britain with an imaginary network of grid squares. Each is 100km square in area and is given a unique alphabetic reference, as shown in the diagram above.

These squares are sub-divided into one hundred 10km squares, identified by vertical lines (eastings) and horizontal lines (northings). The reference for the square a feature is located within is made by adding the numbers of the two lines which cross in the bottom left corner of that square to the alphabetic reference (ignoring the small figures). The easting is quoted first. For example, SH6050.

For a 2-figure reference, the zeros are omitted, giving just SH65. In this book, we use 4-figure references, which allow us to pinpoint the feature more accurately by dividing the 10km square into one hundred 1km squares. These squares are not actually printed on the road atlas but are estimated by eye. The same process is carried out as before, giving an enhanced reference of SH6154.

Key to Atlas

M4	Motorway with number	Toll	Toll	ⓀⓂ	Abbey, cathedral or priory
S Fleet	Motorway service area	▪▪▪▪▪	Road underconstruction	⬌	Aquarium
	Motorway toll	▬▬▬▬	Narrow Primary route with passing places	✗	Castle
11	Motorway junction with and without number	➝	Steep gradient	⌒	Cave
3	Restricted motorway junctions	⊸✕	Railway station and level crossing	▼	Country park
	Motorway and junction under construction	┼┼┼┼	Tourist railway	⚐	County cricket ground
A3	Primary route single/dual carriageway	▬ ▬ ▬	National trail	⬛	Farm or animal centre
BATH	Primary route destinations	▬▬▬▬	Forest drive	✿	Garden
	Roundabout	～～～	Heritage coast	⌐	Golf course
▾ 5 ▾	Distance in miles between symbols	⛴	Ferry route	▦	Historic house
A1123	Other A Road single/dual carriageway	6	Walk start point	⬛	Horse racing
B2070	B road single/dual carriageway	1	Cycle start point	▦	Motor racing
	Unclassified road single/dual carriageway	3	Tour start point	⬛	Museum
⊨═════⊨	Road tunnel			⊕	Airport
				Ⓗ	Heliport
				✖	Windmill
				NT	National Trust property

NTS	National Trust for Scotland property
↝	Nature reserve
★	Other place of interest
P·R	Park and Ride location
⚑	Picnic site
⚙	Steam centre
⛷	Ski slope natural
⛷	Ski slope artificial
ⓘ	Tourist Information Centre
☀	Viewpoint
Ⓥ	Visitor or heritage centre
✗	Zoological or wildlife collection
	Forest Park
	National Park (England & Wales)
	National Scenic Area (Scotland)

CARDONALD COLLEGE LIBRARY 323018 1403

The Automobile Association would like to thank the following photographers and companies for their assistance in the preparation of this book. Abbreviations for the picture credits are as follows – (t) top; (b) bottom; (c) centre; (l) left; (r) right; (AA) AA World Travel Library

Front cover AA/Mike Kipling; back cover AA/Mike Kipling; back cover flap (i) AA/Mike Kipling; (ii) AA/Mike Kipling; (iii) AA/Mike Kipling; (iv) AA/Linda Whitwam; (v) AA/Mike Kipling; inside front cover AA/Mike Kipling; inside back cover AA/Mike Kipling;1 AA/Mike Kipling; 4/5 AA/Mike Kipling; 8t AA/Mike Kipling; 8b AA/Mike Kipling; 9 AA/Mike Kipling; 10t AA/Mike Kipling; 10b AA/Mike Kipling; 11t AA/Mike Kipling; 11b AA/Mike Kipling; 13 AA/Mike Kipling; 14tl AA/Mike Kipling; 14tr Stephen Gregory; 14b AA/Mike Kipling; 18l AA/Mike Kipling; 18r AA/Mike Kipling; 19 AA/Mike Kipling; 21t AA/Mike Kipling; 21b AA/Mike Kipling; 22 AA/Mike Kipling; 23t AA/Mike Kipling; 23b AA/Mike Kipling; 26 AA/Mike Kipling; 31 AA/Mike Kipling; 32 AA/Mike Kipling; 37 AA/Mike Kipling; 40 AA/Mike Kipling; 44/5 AA/Mike Kipling; 50 AA/Mike Kipling; 52l AA/Mike Kipling; 52r AA/Mike Kipling; 53 AA/Mike Kipling; 55tl AA/Mike Kipling; 55tr AA/Mike Kipling; 55b AA/Mike Kipling; 56 AA/Mike Kipling; 57t AA/Linda Whitwam; 57b AA; 61 AA/Mike Kipling; 65 AA/Mike Kipling; 77 AA/Mike Kipling; 84 AA/Mike Kipling; 86 AA/Richard Newton; 88l AA/Mike Kipling; 88r AA/Mike Kipling; 89 AA/John Morrison; 91tl AA/Chris Coe; 91tr AA/Mike Kipling; 91b AA/Mike Kipling; 92c AA/Mike Kipling; 92b AA/Linda Whitwam; 93t AA/Linda Whitwam; 93c AA/Mike Kipling; 93b AA/Linda Whitwam; 97 AA/Mike Kipling; 103 AA/Mike Kipling; 106 AA/Mike Kipling; 111 AA/Mike Kipling; 112 AA/Mike Kipling; 114l AA/Linda Whitwam; 114r AA/Mike Kipling; 115 AA/Mike Kipling; 117tl AA; 117tr AA/Mike Kipling; 117b AA/Linda Whitwam; 118c AA/Mike Kipling; 118bl AA/Mike Kipling; 118br AA/John Morrison; 119t AA/Mike Kipling; 119b AA/Mike Kipling; 126 AA/Mike Kipling; 131 AA/Mike Kipling; 139 AA/Peter Wilson; 146/7 AA/Mike Kipling; 151 AA/Mike Kipling; 152/3 AA/Mike Kipling.

Every effort has been made to trace the copyright holders, and we apologise in advance for any accidental errors. We would be happy to apply the corrections in the following edition of this publication.